Aikido and Rar

AIKIDO AND RANDORI

RECONCILIATION OF TWO OPPOSING FORCES

Scott Allbright

The Crowood Press

First published in 2002 by
The Crowood Press Ltd
Ramsbury, Marlborough
Wiltshire SN8 2HR

British Library Cataloguing-in-Publication Data
A catalogue record for this book is available from the British Library.

ISBN 1 86126 498 4

Dedication
I dedicate this book to my beautiful daughter Hannah, who is a constant source of inspiration to me.

Acknowledgements
I should like to thank Sean Orchard, James Fotheringham and Jo Bruce for their help in putting this book together. I am grateful to Erik Dop for our lengthy discussions regarding the nature of aikido, conducted over copious amounts of coffee. I would also thank Nariyama Shihan for his continuing patience and instruction of one of his more unpredictable students.

Photographs by Alex Saunderson Photography.

Uke used in the text: Jo Ford, Jo Bruce, Sam Benson, Erik Dop, Matt Houlton.

Typeset and designed by
D & N Publishing
Baydon, Marlborough, Wiltshire.

Printed and bound in Great Britain by J.W. Arrowsmith, Bristol.

Contents

Foreword

In 1974, when kung fu mania, Bruce Lee and David Carradine were at their height, I was a 17-year-old who wanted to take up a martial art – as long as it wasn't kung fu. I was introduced to Tomiki aikido by a work colleague and it has been a big part of my life ever since.

I had been training for seven years when my teacher Irvine Cleydon sensei introduced me to his former student Alan Higgs. Higgs, who had emigrated to Australia some years earlier, was the first non-Japanese to be trained personally by Nariyama sensei 8th dan (at that time 6th dan) at the Shodokan Honbu (HQ) dojo in Osaka, Japan. He was intent on passing on the teaching of Nariyama sensei to Cleydon sensei and his students. For me, his approach suddenly gave meaning to many of the basic practices, and connected them directly to the application of aikido techniques. In January 1982, we arranged Nariyama's first overseas seminar, in London. Although a senior instructor in Japan (now the Technical Director of the All Japan Aikido Association, or JAA), he was virtually unknown outside Japan. All the participants were impressed by Nariyama's speed, timing and execution of techniques, and his tremendous but relaxed power.

It was at this seminar that I first met Scott Allbright, who had never practised aikido before. The seminar inspired both of us to go to train with Nariyama sensei at his dojo in Osaka. I spent nine months in Osaka the following year studying aikido for about five hours a day. Apart from the technical knowledge, I also learned much about the history of

the art and about myself. The training was based around a system developed by Tomiki sensei in the late 1970s. The system ensures that all the fundamentals – peripheral vision, distance control, avoidance, balance breaking and, most importantly, footwork – are practised at each lesson. (Some of these basics apply to all martial arts.) Because of the emphasis on footwork and movement, the shodokan system is equally important for enbu (set-piece techniques) and randori (freestyle).

A good aikidoka should practise both enbu and randori. Although enbu will teach the student the most effective defence techniques that aikido has to offer, they cannot be executed with any defensive force, as this would lead to injury. Enbu alone does not really test defensive reactions, such as avoidance, neither is there any 'battle of free minds', since the defender already knows what the attacker is going to do. Randori training fills in these gaps and also teaches the student to spot and take advantage of the 'window of opportunity' that may present itself during a bout.

Enbu and randori go hand in hand and should be practised equally. The shodokan system provides a strong foundation for this. Although every individual's aikido is unique to that person, without a good foundation it will surely lack quality.

On my return from Osaka, I set about implementing the system into the UK. Shodokan aikido is now practised all over Europe, in Russia, Australia, the United States, Brazil and elsewhere in South America, and in the West Indies. Scott Allbright became one of my most enthusiastic students, with an unquenchable thirst for knowledge. He took his interest further by studying the Japanese language, and is now able to read for himself the history and philosophy of the art, as well as Tomiki sensei's research. This ability, together with 20 years' aikido training, gives him the right credentials for writing this book.

Scott's book not only describes the shodokan system in depth, but also charts the history of aikido, from the days of its founder Ueshiba, and shows the importance of randori and how it fits in. It also describes scientifically how aikido works. The book is a combined history book and training manual, an essential guide for anyone practising or wanting to take up aikido, regardless of style.

Philip Newcombe
Technical Director, Shodokan UK

Preface

I have been practising aikido since 1984, when I travelled as a complete beginner to Japan. I had had five years of judo experience and had dislocated my shoulder during a randori bout. I was looking for a similar form of martial art that did not require two players to have approximately the same body weight to enjoy randori. At about that time I was introduced to Philip Newcombe, who was promoting shodokan aikido in the UK. Phil had arranged for Nariyama Tetsuro shihan to come to London to give a course and demonstration at his dojo. I attended the course and from that moment was smitten by the sheer brilliance of Nariyama shihan and the graceful simplicity and efficacy of shodokan aikido. I packed my bags and travelled to shodokan hombu dojo to train under Nariyama shihan as soon as I had managed to fund my flight to Japan. I have never looked back.

This book is a result of 17 years of training and competing and ten years of teaching aikido. I was inspired to write it because almost all of the people who came through my dojo asked me where they could buy a book on shodokan aikido. Kenji Tomiki, the founder of shodokan aikido, once said that it takes 20 years' continuous practice to understand the basics of aikido. In that case, I still have at least three years to go but, in the mean time, I would like to share my current knowledge and understanding of the shodokan system. And that is exactly what shodokan is – a system of physical education that explores all aspects of aikido. Within the system is a randori training method, which

has met with varying degrees of acceptance over the years, both in Japan and abroad, since its inception. It has, however, led to international competition, including the world championships, held in Japan every four years. It is now enjoyed on four continents and continues to grow.

Because shodokan is a system of training that dissects the component parts of aikido for analysis, it is difficult to follow the book thematically from beginning to end. Instead, there are constant cross-references and related areas for each of the component parts. Please look on it as a reference book rather than an instruction manual. I am not a shidosha, or technical director, so feel unqualified to instruct on how any one technique should be done. However, I can inform aikidoka of the system by which players attempt to improve their randori and kata training. My aim is to explain the need for and the scope of randori in aikido practice. I hope that the book will be of interest and use to all who practice aikido, regardless of style.

Note on the Text

When writing, the Japanese use *kanji*, or pictograms, along with two phonetic alphabets, *hiragana* and *katakana*. *Hiragana* is normally used to express native Japanese words and *katakana* is normally used to express foreign or borrowed words. On Japanese *obi*, or martial artists' belts, the name of the art or style practised will often be represented down one side in *kanji*. On the other side will be the person's name. If the person is Japanese, the name will also be in *kanji*; if not, it will be in *katakana*. *Kanji* can be read using *kunyomi*, or Japanese sounds, or with *onyomi*, or Chinese sounds. Generally speaking, single *kanji* are read using *kunyomi* and compound *kanji* (two or three put together) are read using *onyomi*.

The text in this book depicts all the *kanji* phonetically. There are no capital letters or plurals in Japanese and this is generally reflected in the text, although initial capitals have been used for Japanese place names and Japanese names.

There are various terms for players in aikido, and across the aikido styles. Kenji Tomiki adopted the term *tori* for the person who executes technique, and *uke* for the person who receives technique. In competitive practice, tori becomes *toshu*, or 'empty-handed' and uke becomes *tanto*, or 'with a weapon'. In actual competition players are anonymously distinguished with a red or white belt, *aka* and *shiro* respectively.

1 Aikido: An Introduction

What is Aikido?

The term *aikido* is written using three Chinese pictographic characters (or *kanji*): *ai*, *ki* and *do*.

Interpreting *kanji* can be problematic as a single character may have several meanings. Furthermore, when a single character is put together with other characters in a compound, yet more interpretations are possible. In the term *aikido*, the meaning of the first and last characters – *ai* and *do* – can be interpreted as 'to meet' and, in this case, as 'road' or 'way', with the connotation of a long journey.

The term *do* was the preferred modern replacement for *jutsu*, meaning 'arts/skills', and is thought to have been introduced into the language of budo by Jigoro Kano, the founder of modern judo. Budo is the contemporary derivation of *bu jutsu* and is inadequately translated as 'martial arts'. Budo consists of two kanji, *bu* and *do*, the 'bu' itself being made up of two kanji, *ko* and *yameru*. The Japanese expression *ko o yameru* means 'to cease violence' and therefore budo can be interpreted as 'to seek a peaceful solution'.

Artists of any medium know that their art takes many years of study, if not a lifetime, to perfect; budo is no exception and *do* is used to imply this. Another important implication of *do* is that of a system of learning, rather than a haphazard teaching format at the whim of the instructor. The systemization of skills was a crucial departure from exclusive classical *ju jutsu* teaching and led to an inclusive system of budo practice within physical education in Japan.

Interpreting *ki* and *aiki*

The *kanji* of *ki* appears in many Japanese words and expressions and can mean many things. Words such as *genki* and *byoki* (respectively, 'well' and 'ill') and *tenki* and *kuki* ('weather' and 'atmosphere') are very common in Japanese, as are expressions such as *ki o tsukete*, meaning 'take care'. These examples hint at an atmospheric or energetic condition and the dictionary definition of *ki* also covers intention, mood and disposition. However, the compound *aiki* is not entered in the Japanese dictionary and is not in general usage.

In the context of aikido, *ki* has generally been interpreted as 'spirit', 'energy' or 'life force'. The use of *aiki* in budo can be found in *ken jutsu* texts (journals on sword skills) in the early 1900s, and it is described as a coming together of two free wills who put their spiritual mettle to the test. It was used with a negative connotation, and was to be avoided, since emotional attachment to combat clouded technical concentration. However, with the advent of the Meiji era, which saw the end of the *shogunate* system of government, with its supreme military lords and the dawning of a peaceful, contemporary Japan, a deeper meaning began to be attached to *aiki*. It became synonymous with the ability to read the aggressive intentions of another and to displace his energy and strike at his anatomical weakness.

Morihei Ueshiba is believed to be the first to have used the term *aiki* to describe the *ju jutsu* techniques he was teaching at the time. From its use as a descriptive word, *aiki* became synonymous with Ueshiba's technical

11

style. He called his art first *aikibudo* and finally *aikido*. Ueshiba saw *aiki* as the ability to
draw on a universal force that could be utilized at will. It is clear that his understanding
of what this universal force was, and where it
came from, was profoundly influenced by his
involvement with the *oomoto* religion.

Various key players who practised with
Ueshiba in the early days of aikido's development had very differing views on the meaning
of *aiki*, and the amount of training time that
should be given to developing *ki* power. Kenji
Tomiki, one of the key aikidoka of that time,
attempted to find a satisfactory interpretation
of *ki* as it related to people. He settled on
'mood' or 'morale', human expressions of the
amount and quality of energy or spirit present
at a given time – good or bad mood, high or
low morale. Mood relates to state of mind,
morale to a moral condition regarding, in
particular, discipline and confidence in groups
of people.

When Tomiki watched Ueshiba perform
techniques he saw *aiki* as something akin to
that synchronization that modern-day ath-
letes call 'zoning'. That is to say, when mind
and body work perfectly together, amazing
feats of skill can be achieved. This was not a
new idea to Tomiki, who had spent many
years studying the impressive techniques of
Jigoro Kano. Also he recognized that both
Kano and Ueshiba were able to blend with an
attacker's force and execute a throw or hold.
For Kano this was the principle of *ju* and for
Ueshiba it was the manifestation of *aiki*.

Tomiki's vision of *aiki*, on the internal
level, can be interpreted as a combined physical and psychological energy producing a
highly focused experience. On the external
level, the term can describe a conciliatory
reaction to an external force.

This idea can be seen in the Chinese concept of yin and yang, or in the Japanese *on yo*,
and in the *ki to* of the *ki to ryu ju jutsu* school,
which influenced Kano and, by extension,
Tomiki. The concept is manifested by opposite yet complementary forces in nature – hard
and soft, fast and slow, and so on – and this
could be said to be the nature of *aiki*.

Reconciliation for Equilibrium

Aikido can be interpreted as 'the means by
which one reconciles oneself and others'. The
dictionary definition of 'reconcile' is 'make
acquiescent', or 'harmonize apparently con-
flicting actions or qualities'. This is what aikido often appears to do. When a person attacks
with force and momentum, aikido technique
can be seen to harmonize initially with the
movement, and then redirect it, control it, or
throw it away. The aim of reconciliation is
equilibrium. Soft meeting hard and hard
meeting soft is appropriate to bringing conflict
back to the status quo. Since the majority of
aggressive acts are hard in nature, the majority of defensive acts in aikido are initially soft.

An attacker who is committed to injuring
another person will not stop attacking unless
he is rendered immobile or his 'bad mood' or
'low morale' is altered in some positive way.
Aikido is an ability to be acquiescent and pliant under duress, the level of acquiescence
relating directly to the level of aggression. It
is, of course, very difficult to remain pliant
and soft in the face of an act of aggression,
but this is quintessentially aikido.

How Does Aikido Work?

It is often said that judo is the art of using an
opponent's force against them, and it is true
that the principles of aikido are essentially the
same as those of judo. However, this is too
simplistic an explanation of the way in which
judo and aikido techniques work.

The Geometry of the Human Form

Others describe aikido in terms of a square, a
triangle and a circle. *The Vitruvian Man*,
drawn by Leonardo da Vinci in 1487, clearly

Fig 1 *The Vitruvian Man.*

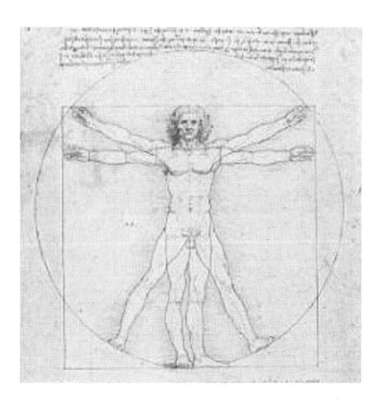

depicts these three geometric shapes as they relate to the human form, and the environment in which we move. Famous Zen master Sengai Gibbon (1750–1837) described Man's physical existence in terms of a triangle symbolizing the human body in its triple aspect – physical, intellectual and spiritual. The square represents the objective world composed of the four elements, earth, water, fire and air. For Sengai, the ultimate reality is the circle, or the formless form.

The square relates to the 90-degree angles that appear in the human form, and in the directions in which we move in relation to others and our environment. The man-made environment is usually based on the square. The triangle is the most rigid basic geometric form; it prevails in aikido in postural basal stances, in

Fig 2 Sengai's description of man's physical existence: circle, triangle, square.

movements away from and into an attacker, and in defensive arm postures. The circle is used to described many hand and body movements – which are more accurately spirals – and also the unstructured free movement of two people moving around each other.

If it were possible to walk around the Vitruvian Man, it would be easy to unbalance him, by pushing or pulling him from behind or from in front. It would take slightly more effort to pull or push him over from the sides, since that would involve acting against his strongest basal posture. It is reasonable to assume that, if the same actions are tried against a living person, the person will instinctively move to regain balance and posture. Once balance has been regained, new weak points and lines present themselves. If the first person then moves 90 degrees, he is back where he started, and if he continues to move in this fashion the effect is linear motion of a circular kind. If you stand to the side of a person and get them to step forwards, you can push them as they step past, and easily unbalance them. However, if you are standing in front when the person steps forwards, you have to react very quickly to reach the same side position, to push them off balance before they can react. If they can exercise free will, the person will attempt to react, and moving them will become more problematic.

Using Movement

A basic understanding of what happens when people move and how aikido utilizes that movement is vital.

Consider an attacker coming towards you at speed. The attacker has used internal force (muscles) to initiate movement and will continue to move in that direction unless he comes up against something (an external force), or applies his muscular brakes (an internal force acting on an external force) to halt the movement. All the active forces developed by the muscles of the body can be described as *tensions*. In contrast, the forces needed to support the body in an upright position, with the feet below the centre of gravity, can be described as *compressive thrusts* against the ground.

Newton's first law states that all matter stays at rest, or, if moving, continues to move with uniform velocity, unless an external force makes it behave differently. In other words, all matter has a built-in opposition to being moved if it is at rest or, if it is moving, to having its motion changed. This characteristic is called inertia. The larger the mass of a body, the more difficult it is to move when static or to stop when moving. A player can use his own movement and mass as an external force acting on his static opponent, or use his own inertia and internal force (muscular activity) to initiate resistance against movement.

If you avoid an attack, your attacker will continue to move in the same direction and if you help him on his way (an external force acting upon him), he will find it that much harder to apply the brakes. He appears to have only two options. First, he can apply internal forces that will alter the positioning of his skeletal frame to resist the movement (propping and paddling) and to push against the ground (in the absence of other external objects) to slow himself down. (This option is seen clearly when a player digs in his heels and pushes against the ground to stop himself from being moved out of the playing area. His legs will be propping against the movement and at least one arm will be paddling to maintain balance.) The second option is to go with the movement rather than resist it and use internal forces (muscles) to alter the skeletal frame so that it rolls, absorbs the force and returns to an upright position. This is the principle of *ju* (*see* ukemi, page 63).

The faster (in other words, the more committed) the attack, the harder it is to return to a static position. It may be that the attacker is not displaying any forward movement, but is throwing out a limb as an attack. However, the same principle applies to the limb; if its movement is continued beyond its natural range, the body attached to it will follow!

If the subject of the attack is unable to get out of the way and is struck by the attacker, what happens? When two objects collide with each other, regardless of whether one object is static, there is always an equal and opposite force applied to both objects. If the attacker has the larger mass, the subject will not be able to repel the attack, but will be bowled over, because the attacker's mass is far more resistant to stopping than the other's is to moving. In this instance, the subject must move out of the way of the line of attack.

If the roles are reversed and one player tries to move another player of greater mass who is static, it will be very difficult, unless his balance is first broken. This can often be seen when a player is repelled by the force of his own technique. In this instance, a player has two options: to wait for movement or to cause a reaction. In aikido terms this means waiting for an attack or initiating a movement that is likely to cause evasive action (1st and 4th opportunity, *see* tsukuri, page 109). A good example of this is shomen ate, when the flat palm of the hand is thrust towards the face. Due to the weight of the head balanced on top of the spine, humans tip the head forwards to maintain an upright posture. When something is thrust towards somone's face the natural reaction is to move the head backwards, which will trigger a chain reaction, in which the hips will be shifted forwards to maintain behavioural vertical. His body can then be pushed backwards with relative ease and it will be difficult for him to stop moving in that direction. This is in essence the purpose of sei chu sen no bogyo in the ki hon ko zo (*see* page 85).

If a player is moving at speed towards you, it is harder to avoid an attack, but it is comparatively easy to continue his movement in a single direction if you do manage to do so. To reiterate: if a player of larger mass is static, the problem is initiating movement; if he is moving, the problem is avoidance (*see* kuzushi and tai sabaki, pages 44 and 156).

Acceleration is directly proportional to the applied force for a fixed mass and inversely proportional to the mass for a fixed force. That is to say, the degree to which a player applies force to a static opponent, and the lightness of that opponent in relation to the force, will affect the amount of movement caused. By continuing the movement through the player, hence applying the force for longer, it is possible to increase the acceleration of the player as they are thrown.

This principle applies in the application of shomen ate as tori first moves uke's head back, then drops on to the chest and continues to drive his whole body forwards between uke's legs, accelerating him into the floor.

Conversely, it is possible to nullify the force of a throw by moving in the same direction at the same speed, until the momentum of the throw has been reduced to zero. This is

Fig 3 Forcing the head backwards.

Fig 4 Maintaining contact.

Fig 5 Keeping distance apart.

another characteristic of ju and is essentially the point of tegatana awase in the ki hon ko zo (*see* page 83). The posture of the two players and the distance between them remains unaltered as they move around.

It is also possible to increase the velocity of a throw by moving in the same direction as the throw, but with greater speed. This has the net effect of accelerating the original source. In aikido terms, this amounts to breaking the balance of the thrower, as part of a counter technique. This principle can be applied in the execution of kaeshi waza in randori (*see* page 140).

The three characteristics of attack, avoidance and use of an attacker's movement can be seen in shomen ate uchikomi, the avoidance of the technique, and the application of waki gatame, in the first technique of the ura waza kata (*see* page 132).

Fig 6 Attempted strike.

Fig 7 Avoidance.

Fig 8 Counter technique.

Fig 9 Throwing around the hips.

Circular Movement

If you can avoid an attack, you can utilize various principles to initiate an effective defensive action against it. However, the human body is extremely good at resisting linear motion in a very short space of time. Circular movement redirects the mass of an object moving in a straight line, and increases its inertia, thereby making it harder to stop.

If the mass of a person is close to the axis of rotation (in judo, this axis is predominantly the hips), the body is easier to rotate. If the body is further away from the axis, as in aikido, it will require more force to start it moving.

This is the reason why it is easier to move a person in a circular direction from a distance apart when that person is already moving towards us, which again means waiting for an attack. In Fig 10, uke has grasped tori's hand; tori has spiralled the hand upwards to raise uke on to his toes and will turn inside

17

Fig 10 Beginning movement from distance apart.

Fig 11 Direct push.

Fig 12 kote hineri.

Fig 13 kote gaeshi.

uke's line of movement to continue to break his balance in an arc (*see* go no sen no kuzushi, page 47).

The spiral is a very important shape in human movement. Balance is maintained by exerting appropriate forces against the available supports. These forces are distributed through the triangulated lattice structure of the body, which consists of a framework of loosely jointed struts (bones) stiffened by ties (tendons and muscles) from which the soft parts of the body are suspended. Bones, joints and muscle structures are spirally formed in the human body and nothing is completely straight. These natural spirals are released when the body moves, creating smooth and graceful motion. Since the body naturally moves in spirals, it follows that a spiralling motion is harder to resist. For example, if you push against somebody's hand linearly, they can resist the force (*see* sho tei awase, Fig 140); if you twist the hand, it is much harder to resist because it is designed to twist (kote hineri/kote gaeshi).

This knowledge can be used to a player's advantage. Twisting a joint, such as the wrist, before it is grabbed will create torque, which will assist the grabbed hand to move in the opposite direction. Torque is a moment of a system of forces, which tend to cause rotation.

This rotation initiates a transference of momentum, resulting in the attacking hand being twisted. It is then much easier to continue to twist the attacking wrist beyond its natural range, effecting a technique. Torque can also be used to transfer momentum into uke's body.

It is easier for a person who is running backwards or forwards to stop than if they are spinning. Similarly, a body that is pushed straight backwards or pulled forwards can resist the force, but if it is turned it is compelled to move in the same direction to negate the effect. This may have the effect of increasing the speed at which the body is moved. Many aikido techniques employ spirals, which are the conduits for a surprising amount of energy. This energy can be transferred into an object or person using torque, with only a small amount of physical strength needed to initiate momentum. This effect can be seen clearly in sports such as hammer throwing (*see* Fig 17).

The effect is a transference of momentum. The initial circular momentum generated by the application of torque to the relatively massive legs and trunk is transferred to the much lighter upper arms. The decrease in moment of inertia between the trunk and the arms produces an increase in the circular velocity of the upper arms. This is what is happening when

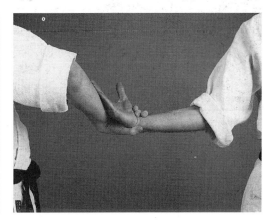

Fig 14 Turning hand as grabbed.   Fig 15 Creating torque.

Fig 16 Both players falling.

Fig 17 A small amount of physical strength is needed to initiate momentum, as in the hammer throw.

'hip power' is used. As long as the arms remain in the centre – they do not spread out beyond the hips on either side and become 'separated' from the trunk – the circular velocity will do the work. By the time the momentum is transferred to the hands, circular velocity will be at a maximum. The feet are on the ground while the momentum is developing, otherwise an equal and opposite reaction will occur, rather than a transfer of momentum. In this case, the thrower will be propelled outwards as well! It is for this reason that judoka who throw using their legs usually end up falling with their opponent. Aikidoka, who throw outwards

Fig 18 Firm basal stance.

The hand must also have a force acting on it that is equal and opposite. This outward-pulling force is centrifugal force. When centripetal force ceases there is no longer an inward pull on the object and it flies off at a tangent in the direction in which it was moving at the instant when the force stopped.

In Fig 19, uke is experiencing an ascending arc on the right arm and a descending arc on the left arm. The centripetal force is pulling him towards tori and when he is finally compelled to let go the centrifugal force will throw him outwards. Both the ascending and descending arcs acting on his arms will bend him towards the floor.

Centripetal and centrifugal forces are often evident in instances where someone imparts force to an external object. Judo and aikido techniques often pull a player inwards utilizing centripetal force, or throw a player outwards utilizing centrifugal force. Throwing patterns with their arms, keep their feet firmly on the ground at the point of execution. This is one of the reasons why good basal posture is essential in aikido.

A spiral can ascend or descend and the gravitational pull will always ensure that the arc will bend downwards. An object that is being spun around is experiencing linear motion of a circular kind, while the hand that is causing it to spin is undergoing rotary motion about an axis. If the hand lets go of the object, it travels outwards in a straight line. For the object to leave the straight path, the application of an additional force is required. This force is centripetal force. It is a constant centre-seeking force that acts to move an object tangent to the direction in which it is moving at any instant, thus causing it to move in a circular path.

Fig 19 Centripetal and centrifugal forces.

Fig 20 Leaning back against resistance.

all involve the application of force to the object to be thrown in order to keep it moving in a circular path for all or part of the time before it is released. These patterns are evident in the hachi hon no kuzushi, and in particular the jodan kuzushi (*see* page 94). If a player attempts to move another player in a circular direction, but allows the arm to extend, the equal centripetal and centrifugal forces pull the thrower towards the opponent and they both spin at the same pace. For example, if two people holding hands spin, they spin at the same speed, but if one person pulls their arms in, the other person will spin outwards. It is essential, therefore, that a player keeps his arm closer to

his body and leans back against the centrifugal force, so that the velocity of the opponent is increased and he will fly off at a tangent to that force when his grip is released.

Fig 20 demonstrates the importance of waki shimete, or 'closing the armpit', when initiating the application of force to another person. In Fig 21, tori is practising hi riki no yosei (*see* page 92), which utilizes waki shimete. In Fig 22, both the cut of the bokken and the striking arm are controlled by waki shimete, which is a fixating power incorporating an isometric contraction of the latissimus dorsi muscle predominantly.

If the direction of the throw is a downward spiral (*see* Fig 23), the opponent is released towards the ground and will need to break his fall (*see* Fig 24) with a roll or otherwise risk sprawling forwards on to his front (*see* ukemi, page 63).

Another way in which muscular tension can be converted into thrust is by the action of a lever. If the wrist is gripped, and the gripping hand is taken and moved in such a way as to lock the elbow, the attacking arm may be used as a lever. Moving the elbow over the wrist levers the body forwards; moving the wrist under the elbow levers the body up or backwards. It is easier to move a heavy object with a lever and the same is true against a much bigger opponent. Once movement has been initiated, the other person's balance can be broken and technique applied.

Balance

Much of the above relates to a person's physical characteristics when he is not struggling to overcome loss of balance. What happens when the reverse is true? A number of automatic and semi-automatic reactions occur when a person is unbalanced, which contribute to the organization and reorganization of motor activity. He has to make a rapid judgement about the direction in which to aim his limb thrusts against the ground to

Fig 21 Elbows in to sides.

(Above right) Fig 22 Fixating shape.

Fig 23 Downward spiral.

Fig 24 Rolling over.

Fig 25 Leverage down.

Fig 26 Leverage up.

avoid falling over. The strategy for remaining upright involves adjustments of the limb forces, in both propping and paddling actions, to arrest and reverse unwanted movement of the weight over the feet. Any change in posture, independent or caused, entails a widespread readjustment of the supporting forces. Aikidoka can learn to utilize these automatic and semi-automatic responses as they occur in free practice, or randori.

Right from a baby's first attempts at walking, humans are constantly balancing. They can balance in stasis and in locomotion. They can balance when static in a moving vehicle or on a moving platform, on a very small surface area and even on a single limb. In other words, humans are extremely adept at balancing even in a continually changing environment and when subject to continual movement. Throughout evolution, Man has developed many sensory methods for maintaining a behavioural vertical. Consequently, it is not an easy task to unbalance someone who is aware that you are attempting to unbalance them and who does not wish to be unbalanced. The two extremes of this phenomenon are clearly seen in kata and randori respectively.

The uke engaged in kata or embu is both prepared and willing to be unbalanced. The uke in randori or shiai, on the other hand, is both prepared against having his balance broken and is unwilling to allow this to happen. The various training methods and opportunities to defeat this resistance are dealt with in future chapters.

Generating Power from tanden

Often, aikido players talk about extending their ki and the use of *kokyu nage* or *kokyuho* (or breath power). Professor Tomiki preferred not to use such expressions, feeling that they were ambiguous or difficult to understand. This is not to say that he dismissed such expressions as meaningless; rather, he attempted to understand them by using a prescriptive contemporary language that was more readily understandable to players.

Professor Tomiki saw ki as an expression of mood or morale and it is clear to see how ki interpreted in this way could be extended to others – witness the infectious nature of laughter or the sense of foreboding felt sometimes when walking into a room. The extension of ki and kokyuho, or breath power, are very closely related; extended expressions of, say, rage or jubilation are carried on exhaled breath. It is impossible to express outwardly with any conviction while inhaling. Sudden shock or surprise causes a sharp inhalation, an increase in heart rate and a disruption in ki, or mood. After the initial shock, there is usually a deep sigh of relief. Clearly, breathing has a big effect on mood. In addition, a massive adrenalin rush prepares the body to fight or flee, while a slow, controlled adrenalin release prepares the body for action if needed. In either event, breathing can be used to control mood.

Humans have the ability to control breathing, which, in turn, reduces the speed at which the heart beats, creating a calming effect. The most efficient way to control breathing is abdominal breathing, or breathing in by pulling down the diaphram at the base of the lungs. This causes the lungs to fill with air, and the intercostal muscles around the ribs, which cause the chest cavitiy to expand and contract, complete the intake of air. It is perhaps no coincidence that the muscles controlling abdominal breathing surround the *tanden*, an imagined physical centre of gravity. This is where the 'hip power' in throwing technique is generated and extended outwards via the torso and limbs, and exertion is maximal on exhalation. The tanden is situated within a triangle that starts at the 4th or 5th vertebrae of the spine and moves across horizontally to the pubic bone, then drops vertically down to intersect with a 45-degree line from the starting point.

Professor Tomiki imagined a ball inside the triangle and this was the physical location of tanden. The centre of tanden drops vertically between the two points of the feet when standing and between the knees and buttocks when sitting in *sei za*. The lower the tanden the more stable the body becomes. To maintain support of the body the muscles around the tanden – the pelvic and abdominal area – must have tension. Within the warm-up exercises performed at the beginning of every shodokan

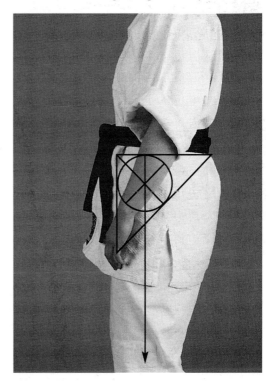

Fig 27 tanden.

Fig 28 tanden standing.

Fig 29 tanden sitting.

Fig 30 Outward tension.

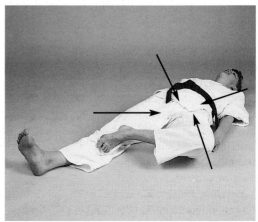

Fig 31 Inward tension.

aikido class, two exercises in particular develop tension at tanden.

In Fig 30, the player has crossed her legs at the ankles and is pulling her legs apart, which creates tension around the lower back and abdomen. The tension is generated outwards. In Fig 31, the player has placed her foot into the side of her leg and is pushing her legs together as much as possible. This creates tension in the same area of the body but the tension is generated inwards.

Professor Tomiki maintained that correct posture makes possible movement from the physical centre, which is tanden. sho tei awase in the ki hon ko zo (*see* page 89), is an excellent exercise for developing an awareness of physical centre and power in movement and technique.

When attempting to exert effort it is necessary to breathe out, otherwise there is a possibility of injury. If a deep breath is held while exerting effort, the windpipe and abdominal muscles are contracted, and this is accompanied by a bearing down. This leads to decreased blood flow to the heart, a decrease in cardiac output, a temporary drop in blood pressure and a dramatic increase in heart rate. With the next breath, an increase in blood pressure follows, there is a rapid blood flow into the heart and a subsequently forceful heart contraction. This phenomenon is called the vasalvic phenomenon and can cause heart attack, cerebral vessel rupture and hernia. Needless to say, it is preferable to breathe out when executing a throw. kokyuho is the correct use of breathing in tandem with physical effort. By extension it can be said that all throwing techniques are kokyu nage. Correct breathing comes with correct posture and correct technique – and a lot of practice!

By shifting the tanden higher or lower, forwards or backwards, the body feels lighter, heavier, resistant to pushing and resistant to pulling respectively.

Fig 32 Feeling light!

Fig 33 Raising uke's mental focus by lifting the arm.

Fig 34 Pushing tanden forwards.

Fig 35 Pushing tanden backwards.

The beauty of power generated from the area of tanden is that it is very fluid rather than static, because it is generated from a firm base and transferred into the arms through transference of momentum. In other words, it is power in transit.

Summary

Aikido only works if a person's balance is first broken and they are propelled towards the floor. This break in balance can be achieved by linear motion, circular motion, torque, leverage, or a combination of these. The effort required to effect a balance break is accompanied by exhalation. Once a person's balance is broken and he is thrown, he will fall towards the ground, *unless* he can regain balance (in other words, restore his physical centre). If a person falls, he will either sprawl or perform an ukemi. Once a person's balance is broken,

the balance break may be progressed into a throw or maintained by locking one or more joints in the arm.

A person who does not resist a throw or lock will continue to move in whatever direction he is put, or will be held. This is essentially kata (*see* page 111). Of course, people who are attacking continuously will automatically attempt to regain posture by changing their body position and resisting. This quintessentially necessitates randori, or, in a sports context, free play (*see* page 153).

All martial arts that recognize the free will of participants practise free play. Free play offers players a test in which to gauge the effectiveness of technique and contest is a testimony to effectiveness (*see* contest, page 51). In itself, randori is neither aggressive or competitive; it is an exercise in action and reaction. In aikido terms, this means unbalancing and regaining balance. Actual techniques are merely the final means of controlling or throwing a person whose balance has been broken using the principles of aikido.

The advantage gained by those who have greater mass and strength than their opponents has resulted in the need for weight categories in many fighting arts, including judo and boxing. Such distinctions are not necessary in the sport of aikido, because the attack is made from a distance apart. Unlike judo, this renders strength irrelevent up to the point of avoidance and balance break. It is the movement immediately prior to and after the attack that presents an opportunity to unbalance an opponent, regardless of that person's mass. Unlike boxing, players attempt to apply throws and locks against a striking attack. Rather than meeting strength with strength the aikidoka looks for opportunities to break balance, and this greatly reduces the efficacy of an opponent's strength.

Key Players in the Development of Shodokan Aikido

Morihei Ueshiba (1883–1969)

Aikido was formulated out of the techniques of dai to ryu aiki ju jutsu and various other schools of ju jutsu by Morihei Ueshiba in the early 1930s. It is believed that it was Ueshiba himself who introduced the term *aiki* into the dai to ryu system of training.

Ueshiba was born in 1883 in Tanabe, Wakayama City, Honshu Island, Japan. He was often ill as a young boy, and, disliking study, dropped out of school. At 18, he moved to Tokyo to work and began his training in martial arts, attending a ju jutsu school in the evenings. At 20, he joined the army in Osaka, where he continued to hone his martial skills, including the use of the bayonet (ju ken jutsu), the spear (jo jutsu), and the sword (ken jutsu).

Fig 36 Morihei Ueshiba, sitting with Kenji Tomiki (left) and Hideo Ohba (back right).

After a four-year period in the army, Ueshiba returned to his home village to work as a farmer, and practised judo with the young locals. Although short, at 156cm (just over 5ft 1in), he had developed a very strong physique.

In 1912, he moved to the northern island of Hokkaido as one of the leaders of a pioneer group determined to settle and farm the uncultivated area of Shirataki. In Hokkaido, he met Sokaku Takeda (1860–1943), probably the most formidable teacher of ju jutsu at the time. Ueshiba invited Takeda to Shirataki to teach his style of ju jutsu, dai to ryu ju jutsu. In 1916, Takeda gave Ueshiba a teaching licence, and Ueshiba accompanied him as his assistant instructor.

The arrangement was cut short when Ueshiba received news of his father's impending death. He immediately left for Tanabe, but stopped off at Ayabe to offer prayers at the headquarters of the oomoto religious group. There, Ueshiba met Onisaburo Deguchi, the religious head. He was deeply impressed by Deguchi and the teachings of the oomoto religion, and stayed on for three days. When he finally reached his family home, his father had already died, and Ueshiba took the decision to move from Hokkaido to Ayabe, to study oomoto under Deguchi.

In 1922, Takeda visited Ayabe and stayed for six months of training with Ueshiba. At the end of this spell, Ueshiba was permitted by Takeda to teach dai to ryu ju jutsu. A senior military official, Admiral Takeshita, who saw a seminar of dai to ryu ju jutsu, was so impressed that he invited Ueshiba to Tokyo to teach.

In 1925, Ueshiba is reported to have had a divine experience; its description is consistent with similar shamanistic experiences reported during this period by a number of new religious sects. For many of Ueshiba's successors, this experience was seen as the birth of aikido. Deguchi continued to influence Ueshiba's spiritual beliefs, while Takeda continued to ensure the sincerity of his training.

However, Deguchi and Takeda disliked each other; the oomoto religion was politically sensitive and Takeda's system of fighting had a non-spiritual, practical emphasis. Ueshiba began to distance himself from both men.

In 1928, at the age of 45, Ueshiba was invited to move to Tokyo by Admiral Takeshita, and started to teach aiki budo to military personnel and businessmen. Ueshiba's dojo grew in stability and popularity, with sponsors and apprentices, and he continued to grow further apart from the oomoto group and Takeda.

In 1942, Ueshiba retreated from the distractions of international war, and went to Iwama to concentrate on farming and training. He left his son, Kisshomaru Ueshiba, in charge of the dojo in Tokyo. After Japan's defeat in the Second World War, the occupying allied forces 'purged' the country of all militaristic ideology, including the martial arts. However, judo, under the direction of Kano (*see below*), had already received widespread international acceptance; many other martial arts went through similar philosophical changes at this time, including aikido.

In 1948, the Tokyo dojo became the aikikai (headquarters), but the depression affecting aikido after the war was not shaken off until a collective budo demonstration held in July 1954. The aikido demonstration was awarded first place. In 1956, the first post-war public demonstration was held, and aikido began to gain rapid popularity in Japan and abroad.

Ueshiba continued to teach aikido until 1969. On 26 April 1969, he died, aged 86.

Jigoro Kano 1860–1937
Ueshiba was interested in the potential for blending his own movement with that of an attacker, in order to deflect, control or throw the attacker. At the same time that Ueshiba was developing this principle, Jigoro Kano was condensing the many techniques practiced in ju jutsu into a form that allowed the same principle to be practised safely in a

competitive format. His work led to the birth of modern judo.

Kano was born in 1860. He began his study of the martial arts by practising ki to ryu ju jutsu and ten jin shin yo ryu ju jutsu. At the same time he devoted himself to academic studies and became an instructor at the Gakushuin University. In 1883, at the age of 23, he opened a dojo, which later became the birthplace of kodokan judo. After analysing various sports, he concluded that ju jutsu techniques were the most effective form of physical training and that the principles underlying ju jutsu practice could be applied to contemporary society.

Kano recognized that his physical strength and wellbeing improved with training, and that his mental conditioning also improved. He was convinced that the mental exercise that necessarily accompanied the physical demands of a match led to a valuable sharpening of the mind, which could be applied to life in general. He saw the limitations inherent in the old methods of training, but he also saw the benefits of adding an intellectual, physical and moral dimension. He became convinced that ju jutsu was an ideal vehicle for such an education and decided to attempt to popularize it. At the time, many Western sports had been introduced into Japanese popular culture, and the martial arts were out of favour. Kano looked for a new name for the art he intended to introduce to the general public. He believed that the fundamental principle of ju jutsu was the concept of *do*, and that *jutsu* merely represented applied technique. Not wanting to discard the name ju jutsu altogether, Kano compromised by replacing *jutsu* with *do* to create *judo*. Kano believed that the judo he taught was characterized by completely different aims from those that prevailed in the old ju jutsu schools.

Kano categorized judo into *judo as physical exercise*, *judo as martial art*, and *judo as training of the mind*. He anticipated that practi-

Fig 37 Jigoro Kano.

tioners would develop all three areas through matches. Players would be free in their movement, quick and strong, and show wisdom and virtue in their play. They should be able to move and behave properly in response to an opponent's unexpected attacks. However, Kano soon found that the promotion of matches to encourage participation in judo led to a decline in the quality of training. In order to hold matches it was necessary to make specific rules by which a winner and a loser could be determined. Once it was decided to judge matches by these rules, players became too concerned with the rules and this prevented them from achieving natural movement. In addition, there was a rapid increase in the popularity of Kano's method of free play, or randori, and as a result there were were not enough qualified instructors. (The same sort of problems were encountered later by Professor Tomiki, in his development of a competitive style of aikido.) Kano witnessed players simply wrestling together and matching force with force, the antithesis of 'ju'do.

Kano maintained that the best posture for judo is not one in which the neck is pushed forwards and the torso bent over but one in which the player stands in a relaxed and natural way. From this posture it is possible to direct energy freely and instantly, into the neck, arms, legs and hips, where necessary. This is the principle of *shi zen tai*, or natural posture. Kano maintained that practitioners of judo should also be able to avoid attacks such as kicks or jabs. The method of holding on to the gi jacket was developed by Kano at the kodokan to help beginners; even then, he maintained the grab should be swift and light, so that it was still possible to avoid attacks. Kano's prescribed posture was similar to a boxer's, rather than a wrestler's. In his view, wrestlers were able to adopt a bent forward posture because they did not have to be prepared to avoid punches or kicks.

Kano did not disregard the use of atemi, or strikes, in his system. He developed a form of entry, *irimi*, which attempted to neutralize the attacking potential of one side of the body, while dramatically reducing the effectiveness of the other side of the body. Professor Tomiki brought this principle of irimi to his own style of aikido.

Kano also mastered *kuzushi*, or balance breaking. He developed two exercises for his students, the *roppokuzushi* and the *happokuzushi*, or six- and eight-direction balance breaking. He discovered that the human body always loses its balance when pushed or pulled in a particular direction. However, if a person pushes or pulls back against the direction of balance break, he may maintain balance. Kano found that, however strong a person is,

if he is pushed when he pulls, or is pulled when he pushes, he will always lose balance. Therefore, the effective use of pushing and pulling can remove an opponent's strength and stability and unfailingly disturb his balance. Techniques are so much more easily applied from this point. The roppokuzushi is an exercise breaking balance to the front, back, and forward and backward corners. The happokuzushi adds breaking balance to the left and right sides. Balance breaking will generally occur in one of these directions. Kano discovered that, as a general rule, it is possible to break another's balance in any direction when he uses no resistance. In contrast, when he uses all his force in one direction, balance should be broken in that direction. Kano maintained that techniques could only be successful after unbalancing an opponent. Professor Tomiki was obviously heavily influenced by Kano's discoveries when he reinterpreted the kodokan nage no kata for aikido technique, and developed his own hachi hon no kuzushi and unsoku exercises (*see* pages 78 and 93).

At the time that Kano was developing judo randori, Morihei Ueshiba was extrapolating aikido technique from the rubric of classical ju jutsu techniques. Kano heard of the effectiveness of Ueshiba's technique and went to see him executing aiki jutsu techniques. He was very impressed and after some discussion between the two men, Ueshiba agreed to teach some of Kano's students. One such student was Kenji Tomiki .

Kenji Tomiki (1900–79)

Kenji Tomiki began to practise judo when he was ten years old, and continued to practise throughout his life, reaching the rank of 8th dan black belt under Kano sensei. In 1924, he went to study economics at Waseda University in Tokyo, and became well known for his judo skills during the 'golden age' of the Waseda judo Club.

Fig 38 Kenji Tomiki lecturing.

In 1926, Tomiki sensei first met Morihei Ueshiba, who was teaching daito ryu aiki ju jutsu. He was impressed by Ueshiba's technique and joined his dojo. Tomiki trained extensively with Ueshiba, becoming his uke, and was the first to be awarded the grade of 8th dan in aikido by Ueshiba in 1940. For the next four years he also taught judo to senior grades at the kodokan headquarters in Tokyo. In 1956, he published a book called *Judo and Aikido*, and in 1958 he established the Waseda University Aikido Club. It was around this period that Tomiki began to develop *aikido kyogi*, or competitive aikido. In 1970, he published *Physical Education and Budo* and presided over the 1st All Japan Students Aikido Tournament. The next year he received his 8th dan in judo from the kodokan.

Tomiki was able to see the similarities in principles adhered to by Kano and Ueshiba in their respective arts. He also recognized some of the differences.

The form of practice undertaken by the practitioner of aikido almost always involved one attack defeated by one technique, although there may be many people attacking once and in different ways (this type of practice is called ji yu waza). Kano's judoka had to deal with a single assailant continually twisting and turning to evade his efforts while attempting to execute their own techniques.

Professor Tomiki learnt from Ueshiba and Kano that the amount of effort required to deal with an attack was directly proportional to the amount of force being applied. A fully committed attack is far easier to deal with biomechanically, with the minimum of effort, than a half-hearted attack, which requires extra effort to overcome. People these days rarely attack once and with formidable power with the sole intention of killing an opponent. This kind of attack would have been used by a samurai to kill a foe and necessitated self-defence techniques found in classical ju jutsu styles. Both Kano and Tomiki recognized the need for a contemporary method of defence against an unremitting attacker. Tomiki was very interested in this type of continuous attack and defence.

Tomiki was able to apply the principles of continuous play in judo to a logical succession of aikido techniques, which flowed into and out of each other, and which were determined by the reactions of the attacker rather than the defender. He also recognized the effect of adrenalin and emotion in combative situations and saw both judo and aikido as biomechanical means of defence, which, due to their acquiescent nature, necessitated emotional detachment. Like Kano, Tomiki saw the sports arena as the ideal place to attempt to control the physical and psychological conditions experienced by people under duress. Also, by developing a competitive format for aikido practice, Tomiki was able to examine the principles and effectiveness of aikido technique when contested by athletic players. Morihei Ueshiba invited Tomiki to expound on his theories to the other senior instructors at the time.

There was much resistance to the idea of competitiveness in aikido practice among some senior instructors in the aikikai (head-quarters dojo in Tokyo). Eventually Tomiki reluctantly left the aikikai and established the All Japan Aikido Association, with its hombu dojo in Osaka.

Hideo Ohba (1910–86)

Hideo Ohba joined the judo club at his high school. Because of his natural physique and strength, he became captain of the club in his last year. After his graduation from school in 1930, his judo skills were acknowledged and he got a part-time job teaching judo at his school. At that time, Ohba decided to go to Tokyo to learn judo at the kodokan dojo. The next year he received his 2nd dan.

In the same year Tomiki took a job teaching public affairs at the same school in which Ohba worked, and became his teacher. In 1933, Ohba began to teach at the school where Tomiki sensei was teaching judo and became his assistant. He was also awarded his 5th dan at the kodokan.

Ohba was a very competent and competitive player. In February 1940, he received a licence to teach judo in high schools. He was also sent to the National Kenkoku University in Shinkyo, Manchuria, by Tomiki to teach judo. (At this time Manchuria was annexed by Japan and called Manchukoku.) He continued to study on a regular basis for ten years at the kodokan in Tokyo, and was competent at several forms of judo.

Ohba taught judo most of the time but he had also been practising aikido, and in 1942 was awarded his 5th dan in tenshin ryu aikido from the Ueshiba dojo in Shinjuku, Tokyo. He went on to teach aikido to the Shinkyo Metropolitan Police and in the next year he was awarded his 6th dan.

Ohba studied several other martial arts as well as judo and aikido, including kendo, naginata and iaido. In kendo he mastered ni to ryu (two sword style). Ohba enjoyed kendo because of its links with aiki budo, such as techniques for use against weapons.

Ohba learnt kendo under master Tsunekichi Koga and was promoted to 4th dan. He was also introduced to a naginata instructor who trained him to 3rd dan. He learned various forms of iaido from Goro Inoue. Ohba sometimes tested his martial skills, and enjoyed competitive matches.

In 1950, Ohba was awarded 6th dan in kodokan judo. Between 1950 and 1953, he was invited to instruct at the kodokan. He was requested to give special instruction to a martial arts research group of physical education instructors from the US Air Force. For one month Ohba taught 30 USAF instructors at the kodokan. Members of the Waseda University judo club took ukemi for Ohba sensei during the course.

Ohba sensei was greatly influenced by Tomiki sensei. On 25 September 1959, Ohba returned to Tokyo to continue the work that had been left unfinished in Manchuria. He became an instructor of the Physical Education Department of Waseda University in 1960, and also held a position as an aikido instructor. He urged the students at Waseda to pursue the new form of competitive aikido. In 1977, after retiring from Waseda University, he became an instructor at Kokushikan University (the university attended by Nariyama sensei). In 1978, he was awarded 9th dan by Tomiki shihan.

Ohba's history exactly parallels the history of the development of the competitive style of aikido and its organization, the Japan Aikido Association. After Professor Tomiki's death, in 1979, Ohba succeeded him, becoming the second President of the Japan Aikido Association. Competitive aikido grew in popularity abroad as well as in Japan, and Ohba felt the need to instruct in foreign countries. He went first to Taiwan (1970), then Britain and Europe (1976, 1977) and, finally, Australia (1981). Ohba concentrated on the development of Tomiki's style of aikido right up until his death in 1986.

Fig 39 Hideo Ohba.

Nariyama Tetsuro (born 1947)

Nariyama shihan started his budo training at high school, where he joined the judo club. He was inspired by the judo he saw in the 1964 Tokyo Olympics and aspired to become an Olympic judo player.

In 1966, he entered the Kokushikan University, where he met Kenji Tomiki, who was instructing in judo and aikido. He became the captain of the aikido club and took on the role of Tomiki's uke. He helped Tomiki introduce the concept of randori, or free practice, in various universities around Japan.

On his graduation, Nariyama sensei was sent by Professor Tomiki to Osaka, where he continued to teach randori practice, and also undertook extensive instruction in traditional aikido, as an assistant to the then aikikai

Fig 40 Nariyama Tetsuro.

Kansai hombu shihan, Hirokazu Kobayashi shihan. Kobayashi shihan was Morihei Ueshiba's last uchi deshi before his death. Under him, Nariyama reached the grade of 5th dan.

In 1972, the historic Second Japan Budo Festival took place, endorsed by the three main aikido groups: aikikai, led by 2nd doshu Kisshomaru Ueshiba; yoshinkan, led by Gozo Shioda; and the Japan Aikido Association, led by Kenji Tomiki. Nariyama sensei was asked to give an embu demonstration.

In 1976, Tomiki opened the central dojo for his style of aikido, the shodokan hombu dojo in Showacho, Osaka. Nariyama became its shihan. Nariyama and Professor Tomiki travelled abroad promoting randori practice. Because of their efforts, in 1989 the first international competitive aikido tournament was held, with participants from ten countries. In 1997, a party was held in Osaka to celebrate the 30th anniversary of shodokan.

Nariyama shihan is currently the shihan at shodokan hombu dojo, and is also a lecturer at the universities of Kokushikan and Waseda and at the police academy in Osaka. In accordance with the wishes of Tomiki shihan towards the end of his life, Nariyama shihan continues to receive many foreign students at hombu dojo and to travel abroad giving seminars and courses.

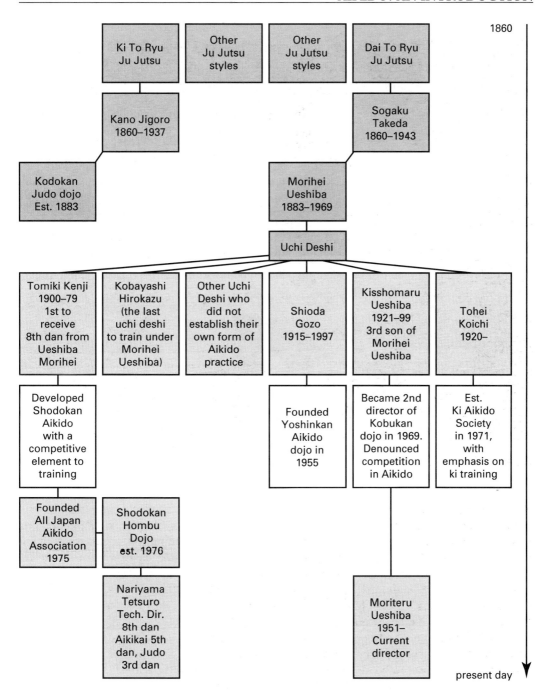

Fig 41 Diagrammatic history of aikido, the Japan Aikido Association and shodokan aikido.

昭道館

2   Shodokan Aikido

Background

The Japan Aikido Association was established on 9 March 1975 as the official governing body of Professor Tomiki's style of aikido. Today, there are many university and public clubs under the JAA umbrella. The two main contributors to the development of competitive aikido in its early years were Waseda University club and the shodokan hombu dojo.

The Waseda aikido club was formed in 1958 by Professor Tomiki, and was the testing ground for competitive aikido. shodokan was formed in 1967 as Tomiki's first full-time dojo. It was set up exclusively for the research and teaching of shodokan aikido. The current dojo was provided by Uchiyama sensei, Vice President of the JAA, in March 1988. Uchiyama shared Professor Tomiki's passion for aikido and his ideas on randori and offered him a part of his company building as a dojo. Ohba shihan became the chief instructor. Murakami sensei, from Waseda University, taught from 1963 to 1967. Uchiyama became the instructor in 1967. In 1969, Hirokazu Kobayashi shihan invited Tomiki to Osaka. Tomiki gave a short course on competitive aikido. Kobayashi shihan discussed Tomiki's ideas with him and suggested he show his randori techniques to his students.

In 1970, Professor Tomiki retired from Waseda University and concentrated on teaching shodokan aikido. He sent a new instructor, Nariyama sensei, to Osaka. Nariyama taught in shodokan, but also received instruction from Kobayashi shihan in traditional aikido. Nariyama sensei acted as Kobayashi's uchi-deshi and was able to introduce Tomiki's randori system to the university students under Kobayashi. In 1975 Tomiki talked to Kobayashi about starting a central dojo. In 1976, Uchiyama sensei provided a dojo with Tomiki as its head.

Professor Tomiki's dedication and contribution to aikido is reflected in his calligraphy *mu shin mu gamae* and the symbol of shodokan and the JAA (*see below*). The original documents are displayed in the current shodokan hombu dojo.

Professor Tomiki wanted the shodokan to be the centre for aikido activities. Today, the shodokan hombu dojo is the central dojo for both the JAA and the world of competitive aikido. It is headed by Tetsuro Nariyama shihan.

The Name

Professor Tomiki gave the name *shodokan* to his style and system of aikido, and to the headquarters dojo building in Showacho, Osaka. The name of the company that provided Tomiki sensei with the space to establish his dojo began with the phonetic sound *sho*. Sho is also the first kanji of the sho wa period in which the dojo was established. The three kanji (on the facing page) make up the name *sho* meaning 'bright' or 'clear', *do* meaning 'road', and *kan* meaning 'building' or 'hall'. The complete term *shodokan* has been translated by Shishida shihan as 'the place for teaching the way'.

shodokan is often used to describe the hombu dojo in Osaka, and the style of aikido

Fig 42 The shodokan aikido name.

taught by Nariyama shihan there, but the name actually encompasses the internationally recognized grading syllabus and all practice that employs Tomiki's base practices and free play training methods of randori.

The Symbol

The symbol (*see* Fig 43) was designed by Tomiki sensei to represent the physiological and philosophical characteristics of aikido.

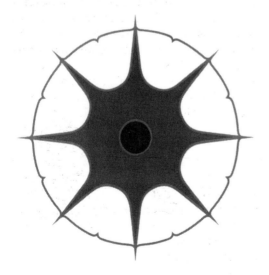

Fig 43 The shodokan symbol.

This is a translation of his explanation of how he arrived at the design:

The symbol for shodokan aikido represents the dictum of the ki to ryu school of ju jutsu 'the way of heaven', which maintains that okiru (*ki*) or 'rise' is the manifestation of *yo*, and that taoru (*to*) or 'fall' is the manifestation of *in*. [In Chinese, *yo* and *in* are yin and yang, the yin principle being negative, passive, female, and so on, and the yang principle being positive, active, male, etc.]

ki is the power of fire, represented by red; *to* is the power of water, represented by blue.

The sun is the primary source for all energy.

Water has no fixed shape and with impassability follows the contours of the environment.

Hence, do not seek pride in all that you learn and all that you may excel in.

Herein lies the strength of the most virtuous.

For this reason it is said that 'the greater good is like the water'.

The symbol represents the functions of fire and water, combined with limitless space, represented by the white area.

The symbol is universally associated with Professor Tomiki's style of shodokan aikido and many associations have adopted it as the centrepiece to their own badge.

The Calligraphy
Professor Tomiki calligraphed *mu shin mu gamae* as a maxim for his style of aikido. As with the word aikido, it is not easily translated or explained, but it carries within it much of what Tomiki believed aikido to be. He described mushin mugamae as follows:

> With a still heart one can access the wonders of nature and by suppressing action one can still the gods of change.

The four characters can be loosely translated as 'no heart no posture', which might mean little on first reading. Both *kokoro*, or 'heart', and *kamae*, or 'posture' (the characters *shin* and *gamae* are read *kokoro* and *kamae* on their own) can mean different things. They can relate to both the physical and the spiritual. The physical heart is the emotion that can disturb natural balance and the physical posture is the aggressive, neutral or submissive stance that a person may take. The spiritual heart is thought or conscience, and the spiritual posture is judgement, which may cloud

the truth. Therefore, for Professor Tomiki, the key to aikido was non-conscious action stemming from a neutral physical posture (in other words, neither aggressive nor submissive – *mu gamae*), executed without emotion or prejudgement (*mu shin*).

The Three Principles

Professor Tomiki recognized the following three principles as being relevant to all judo and aikido technique:

1. the principle of *shizentai*, or natural posture;
2. the principle of *ju*, or yielding; and
3. the principle of *kuzushi*, or breaking balance.

The Principle of shizentai
The first principle states that all movement stems from a natural, or neutral posture, in other words, a posture that a person would normally use as a basic, stable stance in everyday life. This principle is alluded to in the mu gamae of Professor Tomiki's calligraphed maxim. shizentai means the establishment of an independent position. It is a function of both stillness and action. The stillness of shizentai is full of the continuous

Fig 44 The calligraphy mu shin mu gamae.

movements of the living body which can move without limit. In other words, it is the stillness before volitional movement.

The active shizentai is movement that does not impede or disturb the balance and preserves behavioural vertical.

In shizentai, the head and upper body are kept upright. The arms are relaxed and the feet are not moving. The legs are comfortable, and the posture is still and calm. The body is also safe from falling and the four limbs are able to move in a fluid manner at any time to negotiate necessary movement to ensure postural integrity.

With regard to movement, shizentai is movement that prevents defeat and seizes the opportunity to defeat an attacker by application to their physical condition. shizentai is a posture which encompasses these two requirements.

Professor Tomiki recognized three types of natural posture:

1. *shizen hontai*, or neutral posture, where the feet are together with the toes pointing slightly outwards, the arms relaxed and loosely hanging by the sides;
2. *migi gamae*, or right posture, where the right foot has stepped forwards and physical centre is placed directly between the feet; and
3. *hidari gamae*, or left posture, where the left foot has stepped forwards.

Of course, it is also possible to step back one step into these postures from neutral. Professor Tomiki also recognized *jigotai*, or self-defence posture, as a natural posture where the legs remain neutral but are wider apart and physical centre is lower. These postures are seen in the unsoku exercise in the ki hon ko zo (*see* page 78).

If a person stands in front of you in a neutral posture, this is regarded as a passive stance. It is the stance with which players introduce themselves and to which they return at the end of engagement. It is in shizen hontai posture that players bow to each other. After the initial introduction, a player may step forwards in right posture and his partner/opponent may step backwards or forwards in right or left posture. If he reacts by stepping into a right posture the two players are now in *ai gamae*, or same posture. If he reacts by stepping into a left posture the two players now stand in *gyaku gamae*, or mirrored posture.

If a person standing in front of you takes hold of your wrist and pulls you towards him, he will automatically step forwards with the same foot as the pulling hand because that will create the strongest posture to pull. Likewise, you will step forwards with the same side as the wrist being pulled because this will provide the strongest posture to resist the pull and maintain balance. Such postures are adopted naturally to create stability in attack and defence. The attack and defence will determine whether players are in ai gamae or gyaku gamae.

It is possible to 'see' in his entirety a person standing in front of you, but not in detail. At any one time, just a small amount of visual information appears in sharp focus. It is important to keep a close eye on someone who is about to attack, but it is difficult to anticipate the source of an attack, since it could come from any one of four limbs. The best strategy is to focus the attention on a particular spot and 'see' the rest. In aikido, this means the eyes, which Professor Tomiki called 'the window into the heart'. There, it is often possible to read intention. This is *me tsuki* (ki hon ko zo, *see* page 84).

Since shizentai is a prerequisite of Tomiki's aikido, players learn to move with speed and accuracy from a neutral stance. hontai no tsukuri, or creating the opportunity for technique from a basic stance, is one of the base practices of the shodokan system. After each attack or defence, participants return to a natural posture, before starting again, presenting the attacker with the largest possible target area. Any defensive move must reduce the target area, making it harder to hit. The natural posture also encourages committed attacks that are more easily dealt with, since aikido also relies on the principles of ju and kuzushi.

The Principle of ju

Like many Japanese kanji, ju is difficult to interpret. Historically, the weapons of the samurai soldier were the sword (*ken*), the spear (*jo*) and the bow (*kyu*). Fighting with these weapons was called *ken jutsu*, *jo jutsu* and *kyu jutsu*, respectively. Unarmed fighting skills – *ju jutsu* or 'soft' arts/skills – were also developed. Unarmed defence against a weapon such as a sword or spear meant trying to enter inside the cut or thrust, rendering the weapon less effective. This approach could be interpreted as blending with or yielding to the attack, which implies a pliability or softness. However, the techniques developed to disarm, maim or kill from this close range were anything but soft.

The distance maintained between the two players is an important consideration. If they are too close, it is no longer possible to see the whole body of the other person; if the distance is too great, the players cannot execute aikido technique. The correct distance –

Fig 45 ma ai.

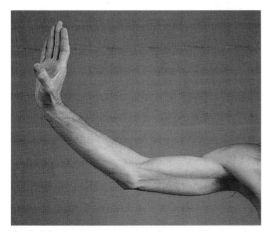

Fig 46 Handblade.

called *ma ai* – for aikido is one arm's length away from another person.

The transfer of power into the other person is carried out through the use of *tegatana*, literally 'handblade'. More accurately, this means the forearm acting as a sword. As with a real sword, the three most effective areas are the point and the two edges. The point of the 'sword' runs from the base of the little finger to the base of the palm. This area is called *sho tei*. The 'blade' of the arm runs from sho tei down to the elbow, and the two edges are the ulna and the radius bones. Movement of this 'handblade' accompanied by movement of the body are two constituents of ju.

The ultimate expression of ju, seen from the perspective of strength, is *ukemi*, or break-falling. The use of ukemi can absorb all the strength of a technique, reducing it to zero, and then help the user to regain an upright posture so that he is ready to engage once again.

The Principle of kuzushi

Looking at ju from the perspective of movement, the problem is when to initiate movement that does not clash with the movement of an attack. Three opportunities present themselves in relation to an attack: the onset of attack, the end of the attack and the retraction of the attack. The difficulty is taking a grip or striking in defence at just the right moment, which may be no more than a split second. The method of using this chance is kuzushi, meaning to break down or destroy. In this context, it means to destroy a person's balance, making them very easy to knock over.

A standing person's centre of balance is just below the navel, which in practice means the pelvic girdle or hips (*see* tanden, page 25). Consequently, a great number of judo throws involve attacking posture by pivoting the attacker's body around that point. The points of attack are above and below this centre, pushing and pulling in eight directions (happo kuzushi, *see* page 32). Aikido works on exactly the same principle but uses only one point of attack to upset balance. In terms of gross motor skills, the body can be regarded as being made up of three segments: the arms and head, the trunk, and the legs. The primary anatomical targets for kuzushi are therefore the head, the hips and the knees.

The Head

Where the head goes, the rest of the body must follow. It is much easier to initiate a break in balance at the head than at the limbs because the neck is much weaker than the large chest and back muscles, which support the arms or legs. When something comes towards you, you automatically move your head, so an attack to the head disorientates the whole body. Once the head begins to move, directing it towards the floor has a dramatic effect on the body.

Ueshiba used atemi, or strikes, to impede an attacker's vision or unsettle him, but Professor Tomiki was interested in the use of atemi to execute a throw. He developed an open-hand strike, using what he termed tegatana, or handblade, to effect a 'blow-throw' (*see* Fig 47). In essence, it is a strike that continues to push the head backwards and downwards, rather than one that sends the head away from the blow, as in a conventional punch. This technique also ensures that the energy from the strike is focused into the target and remains there for as long as possible.

The other means of moving the head is to transfer movement through the attacker's arm(s) into the head. Again, the head is moved and the body follows. You can use uke's arms by taking grip and pushing or pulling, or by moving your own body when uke grabs you. (*See* Figs 48–50.)

The Hips

Since balance is created and maintained by shifting the body parts in complementary movements above and below the hips, it follows that if the hips are shifted out of centre, this will cause balance to collapse. When the head is moved, the effect is transferred through the spine, to the hips, which will attempt to compensate to maintain balance. This compensation then requires the legs to adjust under the hips, to stabilize.

The hips can also be moved by pulling the arm(s) in the eight directions illustrated in the shodokan symbol (*see* page 40).

The knees

There is a natural angle through which the knee will bend without any discomfort, and which causes balance to be shifted over the leading leg. When the knee is brought forward of the toes, the leg is no longer able to support the weight of the body, resulting in a fall. (*See* Fig 51.)

Breaking the Body's Balance

There are three levels at which the body's balance can be broken: *jodan* (high level),

Fig 47 Blow throw.

Fig 48 Pulling.

Fig 49 Pushing.

Fig 50 Moving.

Fig 51 Attacking the knee.

Fig 52 jodan.

Fig 53 chudan.

Fig 54 gedan.

chudan (mid level) and *gedan* (low level). By raising an attacker's arm(s) it is possible to bring the person forward and on to their toes. Pushing an arm towards the head at eye level causes a loss of balance. By lowering the arm(s) the torso is bent forward, creating imbalance at the hips (*see* Figs 52–4).

The arms are always moved with a circular action, which further assists the balance break by rotating the attacker's joints or body out of alignment.

The timing opportunity required to effect a balance break from a grip is called *go no sen no kuzushi*. go no sen literally means 'after the point'; the 'point' represents 'initiative'. Traditional Japanese martial theory organizes attacks in terms of *sen*, or 'initiative', and *go*, or response. In his classic work *The Book of Five Rings*, Miyamoto Musashi stated that all attacks must begin with one of three forms of initiative – *sen no sen*, *tai no sen* or *go no sen*. In sen no sen, the initiative is seized and the opponent defeated with the first strike. tai no sen involves an attack at the same instant as the opponent's. In go no sen, the attack is blocked or avoided and a counter attack is delivered. sen no sen is akin to the Western notion of attack being the best form of defence and a definitive blow is struck. go no sen requires a reaction to something that has already happened.

go no sen no kuzushi is a generic term covering hachi hon no kuzushi, nana hon no kuzushi and any balance-breaking movement occuring as a reaction to an attack.

nana hon no kuzushi means 'seven balance-breakers' and refers to the first seven techniques of the nage no kata without the throws.

hachi hon no kuzushi means 'eight balance-breakers'. The eighth balance breaker added to the above seven is the 14th technique in the nage no kata. It completes the sequence of two high balance breaks, two mid-level balance breaks, two low level balance breaks (*see* Figs 55 and 56) and two tenkan (turning)

Fig 55 omote.

Fig 56 ura.

balance breaks and demonstrates the possible levels and directions of kuzushi.

kuzushi is a situation in which a person's balance has been broken and it is easy to create a technique to throw him.

Applying the Principles

Kano and Ueshiba assimilated techniques into their particular systems of practice that could be executed in a reasonably safe manner. Kano's system of randori restricted techniques to those that could be safely practised in free play, with two players having a hold of each other's dogi. This restriction of holding the dogi greatly reduced the number of techniques available to Kano, particularly strikes

and defence against techniques, in a setting of free play. For Kano, the three principles (*see* page 41) were applied by moving from a natural posture (shizentai) into a position that negated the attacker's momentum (ju), and focusing energy to two points of the attacker's anatomy to break his balance and bring him to the ground (kuzushi).

In Ueshiba's aikido technique, on the other hand, energy was focused predominantly on one point of the anatomy, to effect a throw or constraint. Both men experimented with the principle of kuzushi, or breaking balance. Professor Tomiki was able to extrapolate from the three principles underpinning both aikido and judo practice, and developed training methods that demonstratively applied them:

Fig 57 Two points.

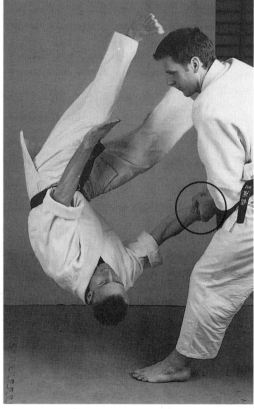

Fig 58 Anatomical weak point.

- hontai no tsukuri (*see* page 97) – an exercise whereby players practise creating opportunities to apply techniques from a shizentai neutral stance;
- tai sabaki (*see* page 156) – body handling, predominantly concerned with avoidance skills; and
- go no sen no kuzushi (*see* page 47) – an exercise in reacting to a timing point just after an attack has been initiated.

Without a practical knowledge of shizentai, players would not be able to maintain strong and fluid posture from which to move.

Without a practical knowledge of tai sabaki, players would not be able to move at speed into safe areas around an attack.

Without a practical knowledge of kuzushi, players would not be able to break a person's balance, making the application of technique a difficult task.

Professor Tomiki developed a system of training based on physical education which introduced and continually consolidated the three core principles of aikido. This system of practice is the shodokan system.

Development of the Randori System of Training

Kano and Ueshiba

As a judo instructor at Waseda University, Professor Tomiki began to record and systemize the principles and techniques prevalent in the two fighting systems of judo and aikido. Both Kano and Ueshiba had already started the process of refining the myriad of ju jutsu techniques into groups of techniques that could be performed at speed but without serious risk of injury, even though their individual reasons for doing so were quite different.

Kano was a great educator and believed that the many social and physical benefits of practising judo should be available to all and not to just a few privileged members of society, as in the past. He also felt that randori, or free practice in a combative environment, was essential if the techniques were to remain practical and effective.

Ueshiba also believed that his aikido techniques should be made available to everyone but his was a religious crusade. In his later years, heavily influenced by the oomoto Buddhist movement, of which he was a devout follower, he placed more emphasis on purity and universality of form as the manifestation of universal love, rather than on effectiveness in contest. Kano, on the other hand, saw the sports arena as the modern battlefield, where techniques would be successfully applied or relegated to the theory of principles.

George Orwell called sport 'war minus the shooting'. Dutch historian Johan Huizinga argued that sport's competitive and sometimes aggressive components illustrated Man's ability to live together harmoniously. He went further, to suggest that playfulness was Man's most significant characteristic; his name for Man was not *homo sapiens*, or wise man, but *homo ludens*, or playful man. Kano fully subscribed to the theory that peoples of the world could unite and compete wholeheartedly in the name of peace. He set about developing a style of practice that could be contested safely and universally. However, he was unable to develop a competitive format that included atemi striking techniques. In 1940, he said that finding a way to do randori and hold competitions that allowed the use of atemi techniques would be extremely difficult.

Tomiki's Format for Randori Practice

One of Kano's key students, Tomiki, spent many years addressing this problem. Tomiki sensei adhered fully to the principles of Kano's judo but at the same time recognized the richness and quality of Ueshiba's technique. He set about developing a system of practice that would enable aikidoka to practise under

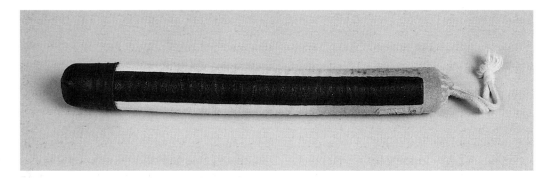

Fig 59 tanto.

similar conditions to those enjoyed by judoka. He categorized techniques into four groups:

- atemi waza (striking techniques);
- nage waza (throwing techniques);
- kansetsu waza (arm joint twisting techniques); and
- katame waza (locking techniques).

Tomiki then empirically investigated those aikido techniques used by Ueshiba that fell into the four categories and also lent themselves to Kano's format of randori practice.

At first, this form of practice was carried out empty-handed, with both players attempting to gain advantage and, ultimately, control over the other. This is called *toshu randori*. However, Professor Tomiki soon observed that players using the aikido techniques available to them rapidly closed in on one another, making effective execution of those techniques very difficult. There was often over-use of judo technique or wrestling and grappling techniques, which lent themselves better to fighting at closer quarters than aikido.

Competitive aikido needed to stand on its own as a genuine sport rather than relying on judo techniques in certain situations. Professor Tomiki's major problem was how to keep distance between the players; he found the answer in the use of weapons. Many of the techniques taught by Ueshiba were based on defences and attacks using weapons, predominantly the sword. This required practitioners to be at a safe distance apart until an entry could be found. Professor Tomiki utilized this knowledge, and introduced a short foam tanto knife into his aikido randori practice; this form became known as *tanto randori*.

The introduction of the weapon meant that players had to keep at a distance and were therefore much better placed to execute aikido technique. The distance allowed the development of atemi strikes, which led to the head being thrown backwards or to the side, causing the body to be thrown under competitive conditions.

Having devised a format whereby a player could continually attack and another player continually defend, it became necessary to introduce practice methods that allowed both players to develop skills concerned with continual movement and logical and successive application of techniques. This form of practice is called *renzoku*; *renzoku waza* are those techniques that logically flow into and out of one another depending on the actions of the attacker (*see* randori ho, page 154).

It is interesting to note that under Kano's instruction many brand-new leg-sweeping techniques were developed in competitive judo. There were restrictions placed on the number and type of techniques used, but new and improved techniques were developed as a direct result of those restrictions. This is also certainly true of aikido techniques adapted or developed to be effective in Tomiki's form of randori practice with a tanto. Initially, a number of judo techniques were employed in aikido matches but, over time, the sport of aikido has developed so that judo techniques became unecessary. Indeed, they are now forbidden. The techniques in the sport today are noticeably and intentionally different from those in contest judo, and some of the applications of techniques are unique to Tomiki's style within the world of aikido.

Contest: Martial Art or Sport?

Tests – Impregnable and Vulnerable

How is it possible to identify progress in your practice? Tests are often used to gauge progress, and the progress of one is often compared to that of others. In his essay on contest, R.S. Kretchmar describes a test as both impregnable and vulnerable – it must defy the practitioner to succeed and yet entice him to try – otherwise it cannot be called a real test. If it is only vulnerable, or highly achievable, it becomes gratuitous facilitation. In other words, if a player can perform a set kata with another player without time restraint or resistance, it is a foregone conclusion that the kata will be completed. Both tori and uke may feel they could have performed the kata better but this can only be substantiated by external and specific criteria. This may take the form of a grading exam or an embu judges' panel, for example.

On the other hand, if a test is only impregnable, it becomes unachievable and efforts will be futile. For example, a player's efforts might be frustrated by resistance from his partner or too short a time span in which to complete the kata.

In a test, the aim is to perform a task more impressively than before, or better than another person. However, there can be no superior performance without the possibility for variance in quality among the skills of a performer or different performers. In other words, there may be several pairs of players who can successfully complete the kata and the difference between them may be marginal, but the fact that difference in performance exists allows for superiority. One cannot perform the best on any given occasion unless his actions are different and noticeably better than another's. Acting in a superior or inferior fashion occurs only in particular situations and a genuine test provides such minimal and necessary conditions. For example, performing a kata with a partner in practice does not constitute a test of superiority since there is no other performance to differentiate variance in quality and the eventual completion of the kata is assured – mistakes and all. The same players may then perform the same kata in the world championships, with a time restriction and alongside any number of players who are equally skilful at performing the same kata; this would provide the necessary conditions for a real test, with the possibility of minimal variances in performance. That is to say, the top three entrants all performed their kata excellently but they were distinguishable by the merest of differences in skill level as 1st, 2nd and 3rd.

Kretchmar goes on to explain that when more than one person gathers to perform a test, it becomes a contest – the word is derived from the latin *com* and *testari*, meaning 'to bear witness together'. It is a transition to a community. Within the community a commitment is made to attempt to better another's performance. Victory is always victory over someone and defeat is always suffered at the hands of someone else, but importantly, to be a genuine contest, the victor and loser always arrive at this state minimally. In other words, the winner just wins and the loser just misses out. It would appear that in contests there is a conflict because two players are attempting to do opposite things – one player wants to do this while his adversary wants to do that. On closer inspection, it can be seen that both players want to do the same thing, only more so than the other. They attempt to pass the same test to a greater degree. A minimum of two people must be doing the same kind of thing for a valid comparison of success to be made. Everyone wishes to be successful at what they are doing and for others to bear witness to their success. Sometimes, the distinction between performances is so subtle it is difficult to discern. Rather than expounding on the mutually exclusive opposites of victory and defeat, it may be preferable to bear witness to the more subtle distinctions between performances. Both players are very skilful, but one player on a particular day, under specific minimal conditions, was more skilful.

Kretchmar argues that for genuine contest to be possible, testing families must develop. That is to say, one player recognizes another individual as a likely opponent. The testing family is founded on the ability to see that someone else can encounter the same test. In other words, a club member may actively seek out other members who might wish to take part in the same test. A club team may actively seek other club teams to contest. A national team may seek other national teams to contest. The testing family becomes an international community.

Succeeding in the formation of a contesting group is the commitment to better each other's performances, without which there is no basis for comparison or, at best, a poor basis for contesting. If two players are genuinely in contest, they are interested in each other's progress during the test. Their own strategies and rhythms, and their relationship to the test, are, at least in part, dictated by the other's performance.

Kretchmar concludes that the ambiguity of the test, with its vulnerability and impregnability, as well as the contest's subtle opposition by degrees, appeals to people who like to operate within an environment of unpredictability. This is the arena of randori.

Budo as Sport

Kano saw the sports arena as the modern equivalent of the battleground. Traditionally, the effectiveness of a soldier's techniques, and his mental and physical preparation, had been judged by his survival, or otherwise, in battle.

The development of a system of budo training based on educational guidelines dates only from the end of the Edo period (1603–1867). The system was adopted by the Tokugawa Shogunate, the last of the great feudal governments. This cultivation of 'the sword and the pen' was contained in the code of *bushido*, or 'the way of the warrior'. It was this code that guided the militarist and imperialist educational policies of respective governments in Japan right up to the Second World War.

After the defeat of Japan, one of the initial tasks of the occupying allied forces was the democratization of the fundamental spirit of Japan's education policy. For the Japanese budoka this raised many questions, such as the form that modern budo education should take, the difficulties inherent in budo as sport alongside other popular Western sports, and the relationship between traditional and modern budo.

In the East, particularly in Japan from olden times, it was believed that it was only possible to train the heart and discipline the spirit through physical *gyo*, or spiritual exercise. Professor Tomiki, by extension, saw contemporary budo training as a means by which free will could be disciplined, self-assertiveness encouraged, and importance attached to mutual respect and the development of a temperate, conciliatory nature. Tomiki maintained that, when sports that wrestled for

Fig 60 gyo.

victory or loss were played out as physical education, they possessed this spiritual dimension, which was gyo. Virtually all areas of contemporary education are concerned with intellectual activity, equivalent to the 'pen' of the old military education; the 'sword' of old is limited to the single subject of physical education. Japanese budo is both an art form and a physical exercise and as such develops creativity as well as physical wellbeing.

Professor Tomiki recognized that all contemporary sport is derived from recreation, labour or military skills. In general terms, the practical values of the latter two activities have gradually been lost (due to mechanization, technology and the professionalization of military forces), with only their technical characteristics continuing to be pursued. Along with this separation from practical origins, there is a natural human urge to push the technical skills ever 'higher', 'faster' and 'stronger' (as reflected in the Olympic ideal). Consequently, Tomiki and Kano did not see the 'sportification' of budo as its degeneration; its introduction into

modern PE culture would mean that its intrinsic value was not lost. The point of conflict between budo and sport lies in the ultimate objective of the activity. When Ueshiba was asked to demonstrate aikido by the ambassador of Manchukoku (Manchuria), he sent a reply saying that he could not demonstrate a lie. The ambassador sent a message back to Ueshiba requesting him to show him the lie. Ueshiba was implying that 'real' aikido would end in severe injury or death for the recipient. However, the ambassador was content to see a show. In other words, for the ambassador, it was not necessary to see anybody hurt in order to understand or appreciate the effectiveness of aikido. Later in Ueshiba's life he became deeply religious and moved away from dangerous applications of techniques.

In contrast, Professor Tomiki saw aikido as a form of physical education. He stated that PE could be divided into that which is carried out to serve a military need when force is unavoidable, as in times of war, and that which is carried out as an area of communal social activity, promoting harmony and co-operation. Traditionally, techniques of budo were closely guarded secrets, given to an exclusive few who were under oaths of silence. Sport, on the other hand, is enjoyed by an international community, its content and practice regulated by universally recognized rules.

Kano and Tomiki set about regulating budo practice and content using objective rules that would be convincing to an international audience. For the first time, budo could extend beyond Japan's national boundaries and become part of a global arena allowing for fierce competition based on mutual trust and respect from a formal educational viewpoint.

For Tomiki and Kano, the most important point in the sportification of budo was that the mental discipline surrounding *wa*, or harmony, must be elevated as the guiding principle behind 'technique'. Traditionally, wa was

Fig 61 wa.

used in context with the practical application of budo, where life was taken to reinstate harmony without recourse to debate. Contemporarily, competition has the benefit of prior arrangement, and so begins and ends with a state of wa. This interpretation of wa also alters ways of thinking about victory and loss. If a player demonstrates determination and spirit, then, regardless of the outcome, he can shake hands with his opponent as a friend, and be admired by spectators. This is particularly true of contestants who are very closely matched. They have a healthy mutual respect for each other's ability.

After the Meiji era (1868–1912), many foreign sports were introduced into Japan, becoming extremely popular. The democratic win/loss principle inherent in them was generally replaced by the multiplicity of the old bushido win/loss principle. Victory was attributed with absolute significance, while defeat meant death or disgrace. However, budo means 'the way to cease violence'; in other words, it is an expression of peace, or wa. Consequently, where East meets West, and budo meets sport, the democratic win/loss principle has winning as its second objective and mutual prosperity as its first objective. Professor Tomiki concluded that the 'fight' that pitched skills against each other must be conducted within the constraints of a strong mental discipline, to enable mutual progress; it must not be connected with destruction. It was in this climate that modern budo, with its new form of competition, emerged.

Japanese budo has changed over the centuries. Early on, its techniques were employed in bloodthirsty battles, and it has subsequently been associated with an investigation of the spirit, attempting to rise above matters of victory and defeat, passing via Buddhist teachings on life and death, Confucian teachings on the fusion of nature, and pseudo-religious mental training, and into physical education, arriving at the Second World War, when it came under the sceptical scrutiny of an international society.

For Morihei Ueshiba, Jigoro Kano and Kenji Tomiki, the lofty objective of budo was to unite the world. Influenced by the head priest of the oomoto kyo Buddhist sect, Onisaburo Deguchi, Ueshiba saw his aikido as an expression of universal love and a gift from the gods, which could unite peoples of the world. Kano sought to achieve the objective through the Olympic ideal, and was the first Asian member of the International Olympic Committee. Judo became an Olympic sport in 1964.

Professor Tomiki sought to unite the best qualities of the arts of both men. He upheld the principle that budo must demonstrate that it is a rational and objective activity, providing a universally credible arena for a show of strength. Tomiki believed there was an eminent significance in being able to sublimate and purify the 'strength' of the battlefield, so that it could be expressed in the sports arena, and he created competitive aikido to this end.

Aikido randori Explained

The Basic Format

The need to be able to decide a contest without serious injury to either party relies on the honesty of the combatants, or of an objective third party. Following in Kano's footsteps, Professor Tomiki wanted to devise a competition format whereby a victor and a loser could be decided objectively. Over many years of practical research at Waseda University, Tomiki drew up the rules by which players could pitch their skills in combat. The prerequisite for all universal sport is that it is safe, so Tomiki needed to restrict the aikido techniques available. They needed to be applied in the heat of competition without serious risk of injury, but they also needed to represent, at least minimally, the key ways in which the body could be manipulated. This resulted in the final 17 techniques of the *randori no kata*.

For competitive aikido to work it is also essential that the principles of aikido remain uncompromised by the will to win. In other words, the desire to win should not supercede the physical attributes of shizentai, ju and kuzushi, or the mental attributes of mu shin mu gamae.

Because aikido is a defensive martial art, a contest will exist only if one player takes on the role of attacker. The attacker (tanto) holds a tanto with which he attempts to strike toshu on the torso. It is very important that tanto is still applying principles of aikido even though he is striking. This means that tanto does not strike ferociously with intent to harm nor does tanto strike erratically. It is the role of tanto to time a strike to toshu's torso when toshu is vulnerable, in other words, when toshu presents a clear target for tanto to strike. Conversely, toshu must present a target for tanto to strike and be able to demonstrate good avoidance on the strike. This is the basic format of randori on top of which all else is built.

This basic format can and should be practised as often as possible. One such format involves a time limit of 30 seconds during which tanto has five attempts to strike toshu cleanly on the torso. After five strikes the tanto is exchanged and the roles reversed, regardless of any remaining time. This encourages tanto to time his strikes. toshu is only interested in tai sabaki, avoidance, and the use of tegatana bogyo, handblade defence, to ward off the strikes. There is no attempt to apply aikido technique by either player.

Problems arise when either player does not conform to this format of play. The tanto that keeps people apart represents a hand-held weapon, most readily a knife. The scoring system rewards the player with the tanto if he manages to strike toshu anywhere on the torso, front, back and sides, below the armpits and above the belt. This reward is not to praise tanto's ability to stab someone but to admonish toshu's inability to avoid the strike – all aikido is based on avoidance.

Players often raise their arms in front of them as protection, making a direct strike to the torso very difficult. In a real knife attack it makes perfect sense to curl up small to limit the striking area to less vulnerable parts and to provide protection with the arms and hands. But this is not a real knife attack. It is a situation in which tanto has a duty, as a player within a contesting group, to attempt a direct strike to toshu's torso in order that toshu may attempt to execute aikido technique. toshu needs to keep in mind that the tanto represents a knife only for the purposes of keeping distance apart. Professor Tomiki knew that the fastest route from A to B is a straight line and so he developed the tanto strike as the best test of toshu's avoidance skills against the fastest of strikes. Therefore, toshu must present a target for tanto to strike. toshu must be able to move from a natural posture into a kamae posture while avoiding such a strike, raising a hand to meet the wrist of the attacking arm as it comes forwards. This is the beginning of aikido technique – correct tai sabaki and use of tegatana bogyo (*see* page 158). From avoidance and defence come kuzushi and tsukuri, or balance breaking and creating opportunity; finally, there is technique.

randori, and by extension the sport, exists because this process (*see* table below) may break down at any time, either because of toshu's inability or tanto's resistance.

Scoring and Restrictions
The execution of aikido technique is scored according to three levels of success:

1. yuko – literally, 'effective'; tanto's balance is momentarily broken, so that he needs to regain balance;
2. waza ari – literally, 'there is technique'; a technique has been applied that is recognizable as one of the 17 randori no kata techniques developed for free play by Tomiki;
3. ippon – literally, 'a full point', awarded for a perfectly executed technique.

This gradation of scoring allows referees to increase the score as a player takes an opponent through the three stages of balance

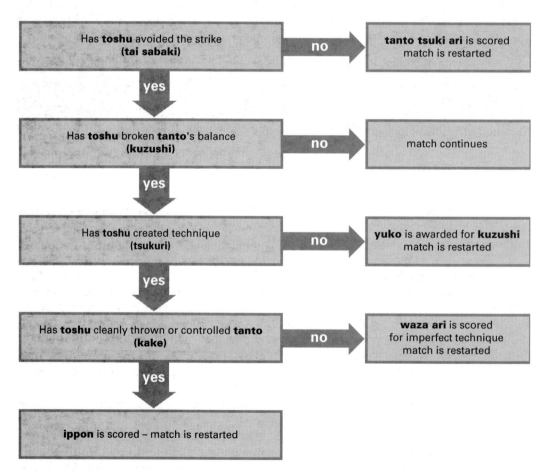

Fig 62 Scoring in randori.

Fig 63 tanto to chest.

Fig 64 tanto to side.

breaking, applying technique, and finishing it perfectly.

To ensure the player's safety, the type of tanto strike available is restricted to a straight line from tanto's thigh up on to toshu's torso, or a curved strike to toshu's side. (Other attacks are performed and defended against in other areas of shodokan aikido practice by the use of kata.)

tanto has to strike from distance apart and has to be seen to move both feet forwards. It is also possible to attack by taking a step back in retreat and then bringing the attacking side forwards one step. In any event, the distance apart has to be sufficient to prevent punching the tanto into toshu. tanto's arm should be fully extended and the tanto must be seen to bend on toshu's torso to score a tsuki ari.

When toshu has hold of tanto's arm, tanto is not permitted to strike with the tanto, as the distance is too close. However, in order to keep as close to martial reality as is safely practicable, tanto can place the tanto against toshu's chest, who has to be seen to attempt to remove it. This ensures that toshu remains alert to the whole situation and does not get too intent on applying a technique, regardless of tanto's responses. Tomiki maintained that the correct choice of technique is dependent on the reaction of the attacker to any defensive movement. For example, in the randori no kata, hiki taoshi takes uke down on to his front if he puts his hand on the floor to support himself, but if he resists by pulling against the technique tori continues into ude hineri (*see* Fig 204). This is an example of renzoku waza.

(Above left) Fig 65 tsuki ari.

(Above) Fig 66 tanto placed on chest.

(Left) Fig 67 tanto removed from chest.

toshu and tanto both attempt to gain advantage, tanto by trying to maneouvre toshu into a position where he can be easily picked off with the tanto, toshu by keeping tanto in a central position in the playing area and enticing him to commit a fast strike to as big a target area as possible. tanto is at his weakest during a committed attack but potentially at his strongest at the point of arrival. The aikidoka must attempt to operate in the split second between preparing to strike and arrival.

Will the attacker in Fig 68 score a strike here or will the defender avoid it? tanto is extremely weak at this exact moment of his

Fig 68 Striking.

strike. He has just one very small point of contact with the ground; if the defender could come round to tanto's left, he would easily push him sideways to the floor. What protects tanto here is his great speed. toshu will have registered the movement almost instantaneously but he will also need to have prepared himself for volitional movement to capture the moment (*see* shizentai, page 41).

kata and embu

Competition cannot be reproduced in the dojo. It offers an experience that is both emotionally and physically very demanding. Its ultimate purpose is not to produce medal winners, but to allow players to gain a much deeper understanding of aikido technique, to learn how to bring their emotions and physicality under control, and to learn to deal with those of their opponents. These are the aims of all aikido. The sports arena is just one part of the learning process of aikidoka. However, the top players are constantly reaffirming and revising good aikido technique, which in turn ensures the constant growth of the art.

Of course, there are many attacks and defences that are prohibited in the sports arena, primarily because safety is compro-

mised. These areas of study are practised in a kata format – a prescribed set of techniques placed together in a group to demonstrate a particular principle or type of technique. Because techniques are prescribed, the attacks can be various and the techniques applied with some force without injury to a skilled uke.

kata is an essential learning aid as it allows for a much broader scope of practice than free play. It is the physical entirety of a martial art, and the physical manifestation of it. Therefore, there are some techniques in kata of which the only function is to demonstrate a particular principle; in isolation, they would probably be ineffective against a real attack. Professor Tomiki greatly reduced the number of kata techniques to an essential minimum required to grasp the basics of aikido. As Tomiki was interested in making aikido relevant to as many people as possible, he developed two kata in particular – the *randori no kata*, unique to his style of aikido and representing the 17 techniques developed for randori free play, and the *goshin no kata*, or self-defence kata, which is only practised in kata format, and deals with various attacks, sitting, standing, unarmed and armed. These two kata constitute a large part of the grading syllabus from 5th kyu to 3rd dan, and span the competitive years of young people.

The aim of kata is to demonstrate perfect execution of technique, with both tori and uke working in perfect unison. This is, of course, very difficult to do.

Tomiki introduced embu, or martial demonstration, into the competitive format, so that partners working together could pit their skills against other partnerships. There are two types of embu: *kitei embu* (a demonstration of predetermined techniques) and *jiyu embu* (where players have either decided on their own set of techniques or are applying techniques each time uke attacks). jiyu embu differs from randori because uke is not resisting attempts by toshu to throw him or actually trying to strike him. In kitei embu, since all competing partners are executing the same techniques, it is possible for judges to decide objectively who best executes the prescribed set of techniques. Judging jiyu embu is more subjective. Since aikido is a throwing art, participants are required to learn how to break their falls, so judges are looking not only at how skilfully technique is applied but also how skilfully it is received.

embu is not unique to Tomiki's system of aikido. In fact, it is enjoyed in most of the major schools of aikido. Morihei Ueshiba himself took part in martial arts demonstrations. In 1942, Ueshiba demonstrated aikido technique at a Japanese martial arts demonstration, organized to celebrate the tenth anniversary of the foundation of Manchuria. Hideo Ohba (*see* page 34) took the ukemi for Ueshiba. He said of the demonstration:

If Ueshiba sensei were a true master he could freely handle a true punch, thrust or grab. Therefore, I decided to attack him seriously. Then I concentrated on taking ukemi for him, thinking how different it was to face a master. After the demonstration, I heard [Ueshiba] thunder 'You idiot!' He

couldn't wait until we returned to our seats. He shouted at me in that way in front of everybody. Until then I thought he was a wonderful and truly great master but his shout made my spirit pop like a bubble. We sat down. Ueshiba sensei didn't even smile. He was in a bad mood. Sonobe sensei, who was said to be without peer in Japan or anywhere in the use of naginata, came all the way up to where the masters were sitting, to say, 'Mr Ueshiba, I have never seen more wonderful techniques than what you showed today. They were fantastic!'

Fumiaki Shishida (shihan division JAA) later asked Ohba sensei whether, when he attacked Ueshiba sensei seriously, Ueshiba could execute techniques in the way that he usually did in demonstrations. Ohba sensei replied, 'Ueshiba sensei seemed to have a hard time executing techniques smoothly.' Shishida sensei got the impression that Tomiki sensei was critical of the fact that Ueshiba's demonstrations had become increasingly soft. Tomiki's belief was that such softness was a way of making the person throwing look good and was different from how martial arts should be. The demonstration by Ueshiba and Ohba received the highest praise because of Ohba's serious attacks and the fact that he refused to participate in a prearranged performance the way he normally would have done.

This episode demonstrates the difference between kata and embu. In kata practice, the ABC of techniques is learned; in embu, the technique is demonstrated. It is a martial demonstration.

One of the useful elements of kitei embu in competition, where a number of different clubs are competing, is that senior instructors can observe and monitor a universal understanding of the kata being performed, ensuring a standard of quality regionally, nationally and internationally. For example, all the senior instructors in Japan have agreed on a basic format for executing the randori no kata techniques and this has been adopted internationally as the required standard for embu.

The best players apply a good understanding of the techniques practised in kata, and demonstrated in embu, to their free play in randori, and can demonstrate it in shiai.

Summary

Kata and randori are not two dissociated activities; rather, randori is the application of kata. It is unlikely that any single randori no kata technique, in its pure form, will work in a competitive format. The essence of each technique, therefore, needs to be fully understood, so that it can be applied not just to competition, but to many situations. aikidoka should ask themselves, 'If I am good at kata, but not so good at randori, what am I lacking in my understanding of aikido?' Conversely, they should ask themselves, 'If I am good at randori, but not so good at kata, what am I lacking in my understanding of aikido?'. Those pondering the former may need to concentrate on action/reaction training, timing and other exercises designed to deal with unpredictability. Those pondering the latter may need to concentrate on form, posture, technical skills and those exercises designed to deal with blending with a partner's movement. A combination of both these types of skill produces the complete player.

Randori is a learning tool that puts aikido technique to the test; perhaps more importantly, it also tests the players' ki (mood/morale). Without contest it is very difficult for aikidoka to place themselves under severe duress safely in practice. Competition is placed squarely in the sports arena but the psychological and physical benefits gained are relevant to martial arts training.

It is, however, necessary to keep in mind that competition can never simulate real combat since there are no rules in real combat. To

Fig 69 Environment, Man, free will.

win a medal is not to win a fight but to be rewarded for demonstrating effective aikido technique in one specific environment. All aikido technique is applied basic knowledge, so players can use the sports arena as one way of demonstrating the application of core skills that may be applied to many situations.

For the vast majority, sport is a leisure activity and should therefore be fun. Competitive aikido is no different in that respect from any other sport. People who do not enjoy it will choose not to do it. But all aikidoka need to be taught the core skills they will need for randori and understand the purpose behind it before they can make an informed decision regarding the level of their participation.

The sports arena can also be seen in a more philosophical way, along the lines of Sengai's 'circle, triangle, square'. The arena is defined by a square, the environment in which the players move. The judges are positioned in a triangle to oversee the two players – in a sense, they are the guardians of the physical, mental and spiritual state of the players. The free form of the circle represents the spontaneous way in which the two players move around the space.

体系

3 Shodokan Aikido Training System

ukemi no renshu (Learning to Breakfall)

The Importance of Breakfalling

Because aikido is a throwing art, it is vital to learn how to take falls. Once a fall has started, the natural response is to attempt to stop it by putting out the hands or arms. However, this very often results in sprained or strained ligaments and tendons, or, in more severe cases,

Fig 70 ukemi.

broken bones. Most common among these are broken wrist bones and collar bones. In later life, as the bones become more brittle, everyday falls often result in broken bones. Learning to break a fall is a valuable 'self-defence' skill, seen in the larger context of defence against natural phenomena.

A loss of balance carries with it the threat of impending collision with the ground. If staggering fails, the fall-breaking reflex is called into play. The fall-breaking reflex is the complete opposite of breakfalling. The fall-breaking reflex employs very forceful movements of the limbs. All other activities of the limbs are suspended, and one or more limbs are flung out in such a direction as to save the head from hitting the ground. The circumstances in which balance was lost provide sensory clues as to the direction from which iminent impact is threatened. The limbs absorb the impact. If the limbs are trapped in the fall, the trunk will be moved so as to take the impact on the shoulders. The movements are organized to avoid impact with the skull at almost any cost to the rest of the body. The risk of peripheral injury is automatically preferred to injury to the head.

The skeleton has two very strong girdles: the shoulder girdle, which protects the lungs and heart, and the pelvic girdle, which protects the reproductive organs. These two girdles are utilized in protecting the body's major organs in a fall. The skull, spine and soft tissue surrounding the gut and lower organs are protected from the direct pressure of a fall. The arms and legs are used to 'absorb' the initial impact. In order to absorb the shock, the limbs remain soft. If a joint such as the shoulder or elbow receives too much of the impact, the resultant force is transferred through the body to its weakest point. In the case of the elbow, this might result in a broken collar bone; in the case of the shoulder, it might cause dislocation of the joint.

One of the reasons aikido and judo are so much fun is the *ukemi*, or breakfalls. Once they are mastered, you can throw yourself spectacularly around a matted area with absolutely no ill effects. Young children instinctively know how to fall safely, and tumbling around is an important aspect of child play. However, such unfettered mobility tends to be lost as early as five years old, with girls tending to be more cautious than boys as they grow older. Once the skills are gone, more often than not they never return, since adult behaviour rarely allows for such play.

ukemi offer a great opportunity to revisit those long-lost skills. ukemi should be fun, but all too often they are accompanied by a (largely unsubstantiated) fear of falling and injury. This psychological approach backs up the automatic physical response of fall-breaking (*see above*). Once fear of falling creeps in, fear of certain techniques that require falls also creeps in, and this results in a build-up of tension in the body. Ironically, automatic protective actions often result in injury: when a player attempting to throw feels resistance, he may double his efforts to achieve the throw; and, when the fall occurs, tension in the body may result in an awkward landing. The Japanese pay particular attention to good ukemi, since the aikidoka who fears no technique being applied is physically much better equipped (relaxed and pliant) to evade it, following the principle of ju.

The technique applied provides the external force to accelerate the person being thrown.

Initially, the moment of inertia is relatively small so the body is accelerated away and towards the ground, so it is necessary to adjust the body's orientation in free fall. Although manoeuvres involving segments of a body and using purely internal forces (muscular tension) can have no effect on the linear momentum of the centre of gravity, or on the angular momentum about that point, they can be used to adjust the position of the body during free fall. While it is true that, in the absence of external forces, the total momentum must be conserved, it is possible to arrange temporarily the partitioning of the momentum between the various parts of the body (head, trunk, legs) to achieve a change in the orientation of the body as a whole. This principle is utilized in sports such as diving and gymnastics and is prevalent in ukemi. For example, in the forward breakfall, an arm is thrown outwards in a curved shape that will be the first point of contact with the floor. This action twists the body into a side-on attitude. The head is tucked under, which increases inertia and assists with the rolling movement while in the air. The legs are brought together rather than being splayed outwards, which would counteract the roll. On contact with the ground, the legs open slightly with the knees slightly bent, so that the body makes contact with the ground at the shoulder girdle, the pelvic girdle and the sides of the feet respectively. In fixating this body shape on contact, and hitting the mat with the free arm, the majority of the force of the throw is absorbed by the arm and the body is raised up on to the feet by the continued but decelerated movement caused by inertia.

Learning ukemi

To learn ukemi with confidence, it is necessary to break them down into manageable stages. Of course, some people will bypass certain stages, but it is useful to know them so that you can check your own form, and teach others.

Fig 71 shomen ate.

Fig 72 Backward breakfall.

There are seven different types of breakfall in aikido, three of which are essential to learn early on. Starting with the most essential, the seven falls are:

1. backward breakfall;
2. forward rolling breakfall;
3. sideways breakfall;
4. turning forward rolling breakfall;
5. forward flip;
6. falling leaf breakfall; and
7. forward breakfall.

Fig 73 Crouching.

1. Backward Breakfall
Stage 1: from the position in Fig 72, cross the arms above the chest and bring the hands down on to the mat in a slapping motion. The flat of the hand and the forearm make contact with the mat. The mat can be hit very hard if the arms are kept relaxed.

Stage 2: from the crouching position in Fig 73, the player rolls back on to the mat and hits the arms on the floor, as described above. The toes are pointed forwards and the hips raised off the mat to stop the body from rolling over backwards.

(Above) Fig 74 Rolling backwards.

(Above right) Fig 75 mae otoshi.

(Right) Fig 76a On knee.

(Below) Fig 76b Rolling over.

(Below right) Fig 76c Final position.

Stage 3: from standing, the player takes a step backwards down into the crouching position to execute the breakfall as described above. Eventually, players will have confidence to breakfall away from such techniques as shomen ate (shown in Fig 71).

The backward breakfall is a requirement of the 8th kyu grading syllabus.

2. Forward Rolling Breakfall
Stage 1: the player kneels on the floor and, keeping the head tucked in, rolls over the leading arm. The leading arm does not support the body's weight; instead, the leading leg pushes upwards to roll the body over the arm. The body has contact with the mat throughout the roll, which begins along the leading arm, crosses the shoulder blades and finishes down the back arm. The back arm hits the mat as it comes over. The breakfall should be in a straight line.

Stage 2: the player progressively raises himself further from the mat at the beginning until he can start from an upright standing position. The back arm hits the mat and pushes up away from the mat to assist the body to rise. The body shape stays the same as when finishing on the floor and inertia slows the body down and helps raise it. The forward breakfall can be used to move safely away from any technique which throws a player forwards, such as mae otoshi (shown in Fig 75).

The forward breakfall from one knee is a requirement of the 7th kyu grading syllabus, and the breakfall should be done from standing in the 6th kyu syllabus.

3. Sideways Breakfall
Stage 1: from the starting position in Fig 78, the player lifts both legs into the air and allows them to drop down the other side. As they come down, the arm across the chest slaps the mat to the side at a 45-degree angle. The legs remain open rather than crossed. The exercise is repeated.

(Above) Fig 77 ai gamae ate.

Fig 78 Starting position.

Fig 79 Kicking a leg out.

Fig 80 Falling on side.

Fig 81 Turning forward rolling breakfall.

Fig 82 Forward flip.

Stage 2: from a crouching position, the player kicks a leg out to the side and allows the body to roll on to its side. As it does so, the arm on the same side as the leg hits the mat. The player arrives as above (*see* Figs 79 and 80).

Stage 3: the player does the same breakfall starting from an upright standing position. Eventually, the player will have the confidence to allow himself to be lifted sideways and to fall on to his side from such techniques as aigamae ate (shown in Fig 77).

The sideways breakfall is a requirement of the 8th kyu syllabus.

4. Turning Forward Rolling Breakfall

The player will turn to face the direction of the throw and roll over the arm, hitting the mat with the other arm. In Fig 81, he is turning out of sumi otoshi.

5. Forward Flip

The player will push himself over his arm with his leading leg and hit the mat with the other arm. This is the escape for kote gaeshi (shown in Fig 82).

6. Falling Leaf Breakfall

As the player is thrown, he allows his shoulder to be pushed towards the mat. He uses his other arm to dampen the force of the technique and throws his legs upwards. This allows his body to roll down to the floor. The player's head is turned to the side to keep the neck muscles relaxed. This breakfall is utilized in suwari waza, or kneeling techniques (*see* page 122).

7. Forward Falling Breakfall

Players should not attempt to turn out of shomen ate in this fashion, but it can happen.

Fig 83 Falling leaf breakfall.

Fig 84 Turning out of shomen ate.

If a player finds himself falling forward, but does not have time to tuck into a roll, this is the correct breakfall to execute.

The forearms are placed in front of the face and hit the mat. The toes remain tucked under so that the whole body is kept off the floor. This gives the body a certain amount of give when taking the force of the fall (*see* Fig 85).

ayumiashi, tsugiashi, shikko and tenkai (Ways of Moving Around)

There are four ways of moving around when practising aikido: ayumiashi, tsugiashi, shikko and tenkai. Using a combination of ayumi-ashi, tsugiashi and tenkai movements it is possible to continually adjust to face another person or a number of people, without compromising balance and posture.

ayumiashi is a type of walking in which the legs are moving one in front of the other. It differs from ordinary pedestrian walking, in that the posture is lowered slightly and the feet remain in contact with the floor. This type of walking can be seen in traditional Japanese *noh* plays.

This is the correct way to move in and out of applying techniques in an embu demonstration, for example. The player is in a state of readiness and balance.

tsugiashi differs from pedestrian walking because the feet do not cross each other. A player is either in left or right posture and keeps the forward leg ahead at all times. The back leg is brought up to the front leg to maintain a strong triangular base (*see* ki hon ko zo, page 83).

shikko walking is done on the knees. Traditionally, the Japanese sat on tatami mat floors in sei za and many techniques in Japanese budo start from this sitting position. It is possible to move into a kneeling position from standing and vice versa. It is also possible to move swiftly and maintain good posture and

Fig 85 Falling forwards.

balance while kneeling using shikko. The player can move forwards, backwards and turn in any direction using shikko. sei za and shikko play an important part in the discipline and etiquette of Japanese budo since a kneeling bow from sei za is the most deferential. suwari waza, or kneeling techniques, are also useful learning tools, since emphasis can be placed on the upper body movements when there is no need to concentrate on big leg movements at the same time. All suwari waza techniques employ some aspect of shikko.

To move using shikko, start from sei za, come up on to the toes and rise up on to the knees. Stepping forwards and lifting the knee, drop down on to that knee. The body stays upright above the hips and the back foot slides up to meet the forward foot, creating a sound triangular base. The process is then repeated on the other side to create forward movement. (Any movement from sei za requires the toes to be brought up so that it is possible to stand up quickly if necessary, without becoming trapped, with the legs tucked under.)

It is also possible to turn around by dropping a raised knee in towards the centre, at the same time lifting the other knee outwards, thereby turning the body through 180

Fig 86 Kneeling.

Fig 87 Lifting knee.

degrees (*tenkai*). tenkai is a movement that allows a player to turn from facing front to facing behind. From right posture (migi gamae) the feet are turned to the left, moving into left posture (hidari gamae), or vice versa, from left to right posture.

Tomiki sensei used the term tenkai to describe a technique that involved a turn through 180 degrees during its application. In the randori no kata, kote hineri can be applied first with one hand, and then with the other hand after a 180-degree turn, becoming a tenkai kote hineri. Similarly, the turn can be applied with kote gaeshi, becoming tenkai kote gaeshi. tenkai kote gaeshi is otherwise known as shi ho nage, which means 'four-direction throw'. The term shi ho nage alludes to any number of directions into which the technique may be taken and is a fine example of the principle of tenkai as it relates to the use of the sword when dealing with multiple attackers. However, the term

Fig 88 Forward on to knee.

Fig 89 Toes under.

Fig 90 Standing.

Fig 91 Toes down and trapped.

shi ho nage does not describe the actual process of the technique and so, for Professor Tomiki, it was less practical as a term than tenkai kote gaeshi, which literally means 'twisting the hand outwards at the wrist during a 180-degree turn'.

A couple of other terms are used in the shodokan system to describe a turning action: *tentai* means a partial turn of the body; *kaiten* is comprised of the same two kanji as tenkai, and is interchangeable with it. However, kaiten is preferred to describe a throw, or nage, because *kaitennage* is more euphonic.

taiso
(Warm-Up and Stretching)

At the beginning of all practice sessions at hombu dojo a standard warm-up and stretch is performed. This consists of a series of exercises that mobilize the major joints, and stretch the major muscle groups. The exercises employ gentle bouncing in the stretches, which assumes a certain level of flexibility in the participant.

Japanese people often practise *taiso*, or physical exercise, before they sit at their desk at work, before taking a swim, or during a walk in the park, for example. It is quite uncommon to go a whole day in Japan without witnessing somebody performing taiso. Traditionally, the Japanese sat on cushions on the floor, and, while many modern Japanese homes now have a 'Western-style room', with table and chairs, sitting cross-legged or in sei za is still very common. This seated posture keeps the back very straight and stretches the lower back and hamstrings. Young children often sit on the floor in this posture, with an upright back and the legs providing a stable triangular base on which to support the body.

Japanese people will also often read or wait for their bus squatting comfortably on their hindquarters. The vast majority of Western adults find this simple posture, which all children find easy and comfortable, very difficult to perform and even harder to maintain. This is because the back muscles and the hamstrings are too tight. Although this kind of muscular flexibility is a component of general fitness and should be developed alongside muscular strength, it is all too often neglected.

Most stretches can be broadly categorized as *ballistic* or *static*; the debate for and against the two types continues among sports scientists. There are four main arguments in support of ballistic stretching: it develops dynamic flexibility; it is effective in increasing flexibility; it creates a certain camaraderie and retention of interest among participants. For aikidoka, the most important of these arguments is its effect upon dynamic flexibility. Everyday physical activities are not static and the activities involved in martial arts are usually explosive, involving a full range of movement in various joints.

The warm-up and stretch at the beginning of each class is a muscular 'maintenance' stretch and joint mobilization, which is not designed to greatly increase flexibility. At hombu dojo, a senior player leads the warm-up and the exercises are done to his rhythmic count of eight. When university students warm up, often the leader will call the first four counts and the whole group will call out the next four. This is a very rhythmic and regimented form of leading the warm-up, which serves to place the participant firmly within a group identity and a highly organized practice. A hundred people warming up individually on a mat can lead to chaos. One practical advantage of ballistic stretching is that it can be performed in unison by any number of people to a beat, which in turn promotes camaraderie. Also it has been found that because ballistic stretching is often seen as less boring than static stretching, participants are more likely to be conscientious about doing it.

Arguments against ballistic stretching include inadequate muscle tissue adaptation, soreness, initiation of the stretch reflex and inadequate neurological adaptation. If muscles are stretched too rapidly they are not given time to adapt, and lasting flexibility cannot be maximally developed. Also, if a muscle is stretched too quickly, it can be strained or ruptured. (A static stretch can also injure a muscle if it is progressively stretched beyond a certain point.) If a muscle is stretched suddenly, the 'stretch reflex' within the muscle tissue will cause the muscle to contract, to protect it from overstretching. In any event, these contractile elements need to remain relaxed for the safest stretching.

Static stretching involves a position that is held for a length of time, which may be repeated. Static stretching is characterized by maximum control and little or no movement. The advantages of static stretching are that it is scientifically based and it shows effectiveness in

Fig 92 Passive stretch.

Fig 93 Passive stretch.

Fig 94 Passive–active stretch.

enhancing range of movement. Superficially, however, people may find static stretching boring or time-consuming.

Practising static stretching only, at the expense of any ballistic stretching, would not be sensible for aikido players. Like all sports, the martial arts require specificity in training.

In addition to the differences between ballistic and static stretching, a further distinction can be made based on what or who is responsible for the range of movement in the stretch, and whether the movement is free or restrictive.

In passive stretching, the individual makes no contribution to generating the stretch force. The motion is performed by someone or something else.

In passive active stretching, the participant is placed into the stretch by someone else and then attempts to hold the stretch unaided.

(Above) Fig 95 Active
stretch.

(Above right) Fig 96 Active
assisted stretch.

(Right) Fig 97 Active stretch.

Fig 98 Active stretch.

Fig 99 Arched stretch.

In active assisted stretching, the participant initiates the stretch and is then further assisted in that stretch by someone else. Active stretching is carried out solely by the participant.

Fig 100 shomen ate.

Although both active and passive stretching contribute to improved flexibility, their effects on active and passive flexibility are different. Passive stretching is preferred when the elasticity of the muscles to be stretched restricts flexibility, but active stretching is preferred when the weakness of the muscles producing the movement restricts flexibility. It is therefore essential to assess the flexibility of the participants, and their strength at the joints where the range of movement is being enhanced.

Ballistic stretching has proved its worth in the martial arts, and static stretching has been proven to increase flexibility and range of movement. The stretch component of the warm-up at hombu dojo is a ballistic stretch, to prepare the whole body for the range of movement it is likely to experience in the practice that will follow. For example, in the first illustration the player is stretching the back and thighs. This mimics the position the body is forced to assume when shomen ate is applied (see Fig 100).

When players are hot and relaxed after training, many perform static stretches, in partnership or alone. Static stretches performed in partnership further enhance a sense of teamwork and develop qualities such as trust and mutual respect.

In any event, all stretching should be progressive and controlled.

ki hon ko zo (Base Practices)

The base practices form the beginning of every shodokan aikido class, and consist of a set of exercises to help orientate the mind and body for the class. The ki hon ko zo represent a practical illustration of all the rudimentary requirements for applying aikido technique, even though none of the exercises is a technique in its own right. The following ki hon ko zo are unique to Professor Tomiki's style of aikido and demonstrate his ability to understand the quintessential nature of aikido movement and technique, and to break them down into a series of exercises. The answer to any practical problem concerning aikido technique can be sought within the ki hon ko zo.

The ki hon ko zo should be looked upon as the tools for learning aikido. There are also some elements of aikido that are repeated in some or all of the practices. For example, both sho tei awase and hi riki no yo sei are practices that develop to itsu ryoku, or the ability to focus all energy into one point; sei chu sen no bogyo, ga sho uke and tegatana no bogyo all develop an awareness of physical centre, which is essential to all aikido; tegatana awase develops ma ai and me tsuke, or distance apart and eye contact, respectively. These themes are learned almost passively while practising the ki hon ko zo, and all the skills learned during the beginning of the class should be taken into subsequent practice, regardless of its content.

Fig 101 shi zen tai.

Fig 102 Forward movement.

Fig 103 Side movement.

The ki hon ko zo are practised as follows.

unsoku

unsoku literally means 'to move with the feet'. Professor Tomiki devised a small, precise exercise that teaches the aikidoka to move in eight directions around a central point. Aikido employs a method of movement that lowers the centre of gravity, giving greater balance.

Following the shi zen tai no ri (natural posture) principle, the player stands with feet hip-width apart, and knees slightly bent.

The first movements are forward and back, in left posture and then right posture.

As the player moves forwards, he keeps the shoulders and hips facing directly forward. The forward foot faces forward, and the back foot is at a 45-degree angle. There is a single foot's distance between the heels, and the feet remain hip-width apart throughout the movement. The movement stems from the

Fig 104 Forward corner movement.

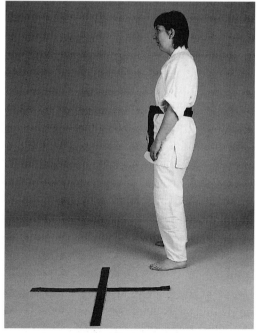

Fig 105 Backward corner movement.

hips; the player should feel that he is falling slightly forward, keeping the back upright, due to the dropping of the posture. The feet then 'catch the hips up'.

The player moves forwards, back, backwards and forwards in left posture, to arrive back at the central point, before changing to right posture and repeating the sequence. This sequence of movement is the footwork used in tegatana awase (see page 83).

The second direction is to the side of centre.

Again, starting from neutral, the player moves to the left, right, right and then left, and back to centre. On moving sideways, the movement is again initiated from the hips with the feet 'catching the hips up'. This generates faster movement than trying to step to the side and then drag the body across. Again, it is important to keep the feet hip-width apart and the knees soft on arrival, so that there is a stable base. The resultant posture is ji go tai, or self-defensive posture.

The third direction is the corner.

Movement is to the forward left corner, forward right corner, left backward corner and right backward corner, away from centre. The same principles apply to the corner movements, and the whole body is turned 90 degrees from centre. The player faces the new direction and the feet are hip-width apart.

The forward, backward, sideways and corner movements correspond to the eight directions stemming out from centre, which are illustrated in the shodokan logo.

When performing these basic exercises in body handling, players should pay particular attention to the feet and make sure to face in the new directions during the movement. The movement is initiated by a count of 1 to 8, which can be used as a cue to which to respond, thereby sharpening the reflexes. When practising this exercise, the count should not be rushed. It is far better to slow the count and move as fast as possible in correct posture than to rush the movement. This

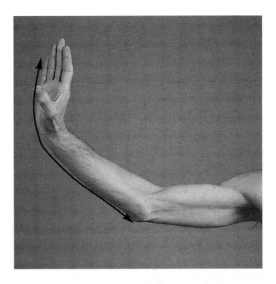

Fig 106 tegatana handblade.

Note

This exercise is sometimes misleadingly referred to as tandoku undo. In fact, tandoku undo means 'individual practice', which relates to any exercise undertaken independently.

---

also allows a beginner to benefit as much from the exercise as a competent player.

This exercise is a requirement of the 8th kyu grading syllabus.

tegatana dosa

tegatana go dosa means the five ways of structuring handblade movements. Professor Tomiki described tegatana as stemming from the tip of the little finger all the way down the forearm to just above the elbow. The whole of this tegatana can be used in both defence and application of technique (see Fig 4, page 16).

There are actually seven movements in this exercise, but the first two and the last two are combined, making five in total. The movements are all based on sword striking movements (see Figs 107–118). When practising

Fig 107 Cutting down.

Fig 108 Cutting up to throat.

Fig 109 To side of head.

Fig 110 To other side of head.

(Above) Fig 111 Cutting outwards.

(Above right) Fig 112 Cutting inwards.

the movements, imagining a person standing in front of you helps to orientate the movements in terms of height and direction. However, they are not striking blows in their own right since the sword is absent and players should, therefore, try not to use strong, chopping actions; instead, the actions should be smooth and flowing, as this will dramatically improve aikido technique. The five movements are used in the kumi tachi (literally 'coming together of swords'), and relate to sword vs sword in the 3rd dan syllabus section of the goshin no kata (*see* page 168).

The first pair of movements relate to a strike ascending and descending towards an imaginary person's head accompanied by forward movement, withdrawing to come forwards again to strike to the throat, then returning to a neutral position.

Fig 113 Cutting across.

Fig 114 Cutting across.

Fig 115 Pivoting.

Fig 116 Cutting down.

Fig 117 Avoiding to side.

The second pair of movements relate to a strike to the side of the imaginary person's head; the handblade then travels around the head, to strike the other side of the head.

The third movement relates to a mid-level thrust across the ribs, on both sides.

The fourth movement relates to a slashing movement across the torso, in both directions.

The fifth pair of movements relate to the ability to strike in one direction and then turn 180 degrees and cut again; and to the ability to avoid a strike, by moving to the side, while raising the sword up to cut the attacker.

The tegatana dosa is a requirement of the 7th kyu syllabus.

tegatana awase

For this exercise, tegatana means the outside base of the palm, or sho tei. The basic skills developed in this exercise are tsugi ashi, ma ai and me tsuki.

In tsugi ashi, the feet do not pass each other, but the person slides forward, keeping one foot forward of the other. The balls of the feet

Fig 118 Cutting down.

Fig 119 tegatana awase.

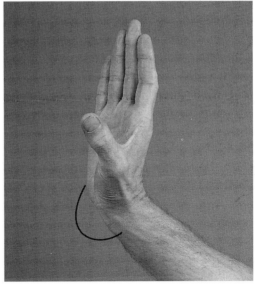

Fig 120 sho tei.

83

ma ai and me tsuki

Since this is the first exercise in which two players work together, it is important to introduce the principles of ma ai and me tsuki.

ma ai means 'distance apart', and tegatana awase represents the correct distance apart for two players to attempt aikido technique. All martial arts have their own ideal distance from which to apply their technique with optimum effectiveness and efficiency. tegatana awase is an essential exercise for learning the distance required for aikido. The distance relates specifically to the length of the player's outstretched arm when the fingers point to the ceiling.

There is no leader and follower in tegatana awase; both players are attempting to react to the movements of the other. To do this effectively, both players need to be 'receptive' and the receptive point is where the sho tei touch. Players should remain as relaxed and soft as possible. A good way to practise this exercise is for one of the players to close their eyes. If the 'blind' player is 'receptive', he will know where to follow. All aikido should ideally be attempted with this degree of 'receptiveness'.

Another means of 'receptiveness' is me tsuki, which means eye contact. Different martial arts have different points of visual contact when practising. Aikido places this point at face level – while looking towards this point it should be possible to see all the limbs of your opponent. (Of course, this will be true only if ma ai distance is correct.) In correct me tsuki, the player should not stare at the other or look them in the eye. The face is merely a focal point from which the whole body can be seen using peripheral vision. Since aikido is an acquiescent art, players should always attempt to adopt a passive stance (mu shin) when receiving an attack. It is essential that players always maintain eye contact throughout any aikido action. In randori free play one player may strike the back of the other's torso, demonstrating that in combat you should never take your eyes off an opponent, even for a moment.

Since all aikido technique is based on a multiple attack, tori never places himself on the floor or compromises his posture, but can always move quickly in any direction. Therefore, peripheral vision should spread beyond the player being dealt with. This 'awareness' is part of the definition of aikido, demonstrating an ability to discern mood, which is often a prelude to action.

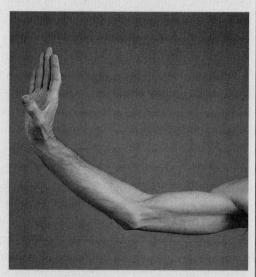

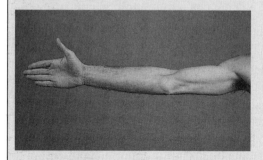

Fig 121 Straight arm.

Fig 122 tegatana.

remain in contact with the floor. The forward foot points forward and the back foot is at 45 degrees, to provide a stable base. The exercise involves two players moving forwards and backwards using tsugi ashi while maintaining a light touch at each other's sho tei. The outside base of the palms are the only parts touching, the fingers are closed and pointing straight up to the ceiling. The players' shoulders and hips are parallel to each other throughout the exercise and the arm and hand stay in centre the whole time.

sei chu sen no bogyo

sei chu sen is the central line through the body, from the top of the head down between the legs. bogyo means 'defence', and this exercise demonstrates the way to keep centre and defend it. Most of the body's vital points are along, or close to, this central line, and when the body is under attack it naturally closes in to protect its centre. The arms are the best natural form of defence for the centre, so aikido creates a physical barrier with the arms. sei chu sen no bogyo, ga sho uke and tegatana no bogyo all demonstrate this defence.

sei chu sen no bogyo is an exercise that develops timing for entering in to an attack. It stems from tegatana awase, and relies on one player simulating an attack. This attack is specific to the exercise. All attacks of a physical nature begin with a change in posture, so that power can be generated from a stronger base. Players watch for this change in posture and, as the player raises his arm in a simulated attack, he will also be leaning back slightly as a prelude to forward movement. Exactly at this moment, tori moves in, placing tegatana against the chest and driving forward from the hips to drive uke backwards. uke must allow his leading arm to fold on to his chest as tori pushes forward, because tegatana awase is only a point of reference, and would not, in reality, be present.

This exercise is done left and right.

Fig 123 sei chu sen.

Fig 124 Preparing to attack.

Fig 125 Entering in.

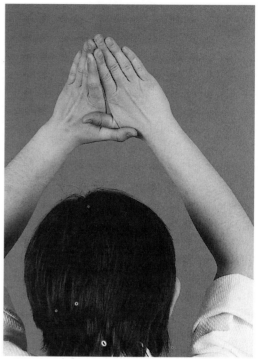

Fig 126 ga sho hand position.

ga sho uke

This exercise further develops sei chu sen no bogyo. ga sho relates to the clapping of hands associated with Buddhist prayer. In this case, it illustrates the use of two tegatana placed together to form a triangle. The thumbs are crossed at the back and the index fingers are seamed together.

Players stand ma ai distance apart, and one player steps forwards to strike yokomen, gyakumen or keri.

Both attacks with the arm are movements that come from the outside of centre to the side of the head (*see* tegatana dosa, page 80). Hence, it is possible to enter into the attack in a straight line. From a natural stance, players step forwards, placing their hands in ga sho and raising them to just in front of the attacker's face.

It is essential that the attacker can no longer see tori and this will encourage uke to take a step back to recover advantage. At this point, tori also steps back, bringing the arms back down to the sides. Regardless of the side from which the attack stems, tori moves in the same way. The slightly oval shape created by the arms will pick up either attack.

In the case of keri, or a kick, the exercise assumes that the majority of martial arts kicks stem from centre and come from a raised knee.

tori enters in the same way, but places ga sho on top of the knee or thigh. Of course, ga sho must connect with the rising knee before it reaches 90 degrees, so that all subsequent kicks from a bent knee are neutralized. Also, eye contact should be maintained, and the back kept straight so that there is weight behind the arms.

Fig 127 yokomen uchi.

Fig 128 gyakumen uchi.

Fig 129 keri.

Fig 130 yokomen uchi defence.

Fig 131 gyakumen uchi defence.

Fig 132 keri defence.

The curvature of the arms when together in ga sho can be raised above the head and lowered to the groin, creating a very strong protective barrier for all the vital points of the body. It also emulates a sword cutting action; when repeated, this will greatly enhance the strength of this defence (*see* suburi, page 168).

tegatana no bogyo
This exercise is a continuation of ga sho uke. Where ga sho uke develops central alignment, entry and defence, tegatana no bogyo uses a single arm in preparation to taking grip and applying technique. The attacks are the same as for ga sho uke but tori enters in with one arm, using the same movement as the third handblade movement of tegatana dosa, and ensures that the leg on the same side as

the arm also moves forwards. As with ga sho uke, the tegatana handblade is placed in front of the face. yokomen uchi and gyakumen uchi are met with either the left or right arm, thumb pointing down and palm across the face, or palm up and fingers pointing towards the face respectively.

In the case of gyakumen uchi, the tegatana handblade contacts the tricep in the slowest part of the attack. It is the curve in the arm movement that 'picks up' the attack. It is not a block, but a circular action of the forearm, which deflects or redirects the strike upwards. There is only sufficient avoidance to move away from the focal point of the attack, which in this instance is the side of the head.

For keri, or kick, the same applies as ga sho uke, but one tegatana blade is used. It is essential that the side of tegatana, below the

Fig 133 yokomen uchi tegatana defence.

Fig 134 gyakumen uchi tegatana defence.

little finger, contacts with the thigh, otherwise the fingers can be forced back.

Where ga sho uke blocks the kick before it develops, tegatana no bogyo can allow for the kick to continue up the outside of the arm.

sho tei awase

The next two exercises develop to itsu ryoku, which is the ability to focus energy at one point. sho tei awase literally means 'joining the hands together at the base of the palms'. sho tei is the strongest point on the hand for pushing and is utilized in both atemi waza and kansetsu waza.

Players stand with arms extended and sho tei placed together. The fingers point up to the ceiling and away from the sho tei, so that the push does not transfer into the fingers, which results in gripping and a reliance upon upper body strength.

Fig 135a keri tegatana defence.

Fig 135b shomen ate.

Fig 135c gyakugamae ate.

Fig 136 sho tei pushing.

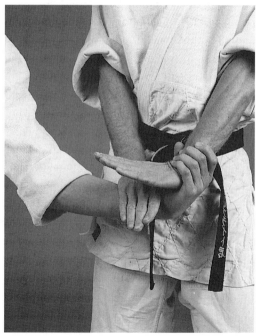

Fig 137 sho tei pulling.

Fig 138 sho tei awase.

The tendency is for the hips to rotate slightly during the push, which throws central alignment out. Therefore, for this exercise the opposite leg is forward, to ensure a square posture throughout the exercise. Players push one another back and forth; the push stems from tanden, or anatomical centre, and is transferred through the arm into uke. During the push, the posture is lowered but the arm stays in line with the chest. This creates a slight downward push.

The exercise develops strength in technique while maintaining good posture. It also helps the player to learn how to root himself to the floor, but at the same time remaining soft. As the player is pushed backwards, he sinks his weight and sends the force of the push through his arm, down through the centre of the torso and between the legs, into the floor. Both legs are slightly bent and the weight is equally distributed between them. In this way, strength is developed in both attack and defence.

Fig 139 Stance for sho tei awase.

Fig 140 Pushing from hips.

Fig 141 Two-hand grip from behind.

Fig 142 Lifting the elbow.

Fig 143 Neutralizing lift.

hi riki no yo sei

This is the second exercise to utilize to itsu ryoku. hi riki no yo sei is the ability to neutralize power. A player stands in kamae with his back to uke and offers the arm to be grabbed on the same side as the back leg.

uke grabs tori's forearm with both hands in a circular grip and attempts to force the arm up the back.

tori attempts to neutralize this action. As soon as he feels the grip on his fisted arm, tori opens the hand, fingers pointing straight down, and employs waki shimete.

waki shimete means 'to close the armpit', and can be thought of as pinning the arm to the side of the body. As he does this, tori also lowers his posture. This combined action should make it impossible for uke to lift the arm. The hips are pushed slightly forwards and the legs bent, so that, should uke release the grip suddenly, tori will not stumble back. From this position, tori rotates the hips away from uke and takes a step towards him. The other hand is placed close to the gripped hand and the fingers are raised into tegatana shape.

Rather than pushing towards uke's arms, the hands are first lowered and then raised up and forwards in an arc, until the hands are at eye level. tori steps down the side of uke to break balance.

hachi hon no kuzushi or go no sen no kuzushi

This is an exercise in balance breaking at three levels: jodan, chudan and gedan, from aigamae and gyakugamae katate dori grips, and from ko ho ryote dori.

The hachi hon no kuzushi is practised in the following order:

1. jodan kuzushi
(a) aigamae katate dori
(b) gyakugamae katate dori

Fig 144 Rotating into uke.

aigamae katate dori jodan kuzushi

As uke steps forwards to grab tori's wrist, tori twists his wrist so that his palm faces downwards. As the grip comes on to the wrist, tori twists it the other way so the palm is uppermost and the edge of the little finger and palm (tegatana) are cutting into the underside of uke's wrist. The combination of raising the gripped hand in this way and moving backwards raises uke on to his toes, breaking his balance forwards and upwards.

gyakugamae katate dori jodan kuzushi

As uke steps forwards to grab tori's wrist, tori twists his wrist so that his palm is uppermost. As the grip comes on, tori twists his wrist the other way so that his palm is now facing away from him and, as before, the edge of the little finger and palm are cutting into the underside of uke's wrist. The effect is the same as above. It is important that on leaning back and start-

Fig 145 Pushing through.

Fig 146 jodan aigamae katate dori.

Fig 147 jodan gyakugamae katate dori.

Fig 148 chudan aigamae katate dori.

Fig 149 chudan gyakugamae katate dori.

Fig 150 gedan aigamae katate dori.

Fig 151 gedan gyakugamae katate dori.

ing to move backwards the armpit is closed (waki shimete, *see* page 22).

2. chudan kuzushi
(a) aigamae katate dori
(b) gyakugamae katate dori

aigamae katate dori chudan kuzushi

As uke steps forward to grip tori's wrist, tori twists his wrist so that his palm faces right and the thumb is pointed down. As the grip comes on, tori twists the wrist back so that the thumb is uppermost. tori steps down uke's gripping side with the same foot as the side grabbed.

The combination of the wrist twist, stepping down the side and waki shimete will allow tori to move down the side of uke and break balance by raising his tegatana hand towards uke's head while turning his hips.

Remember that power is always generated from around the hips (tanden).

gyakugamae katate dori chudan kuzushi

As uke steps forwards to grab tori's wrist, tori turns his wrist so that the palm is uppermost. As the grab comes on, tori reverses the twist, closes the armpit and steps down the side of uke's gripping side. As described above, the tegatana hand is raised towards uke's head and their balance is broken at chudan level as tori turns his hips.

3. gedan kuzushi
(a) aigamae katate dori
(b) gyakugamae katate dori

aigamae katate dori gedan kuzushi

As uke steps forwards to grab tori's wrist, tori

Fig 152 ko ho ryote dori omote waza.

Fig 153 ko ho ryote dori ura waza.

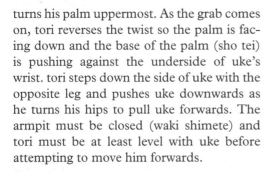

turns his palm uppermost. As the grab comes on, tori reverses the twist so the palm is facing down and the base of the palm (sho tei) is pushing against the underside of uke's wrist. tori steps down the side of uke with the opposite leg and pushes uke downwards as he turns his hips to pull uke forwards. The armpit must be closed (waki shimete) and tori must be at least level with uke before attempting to move him forwards.

gyakugamae katate dori gedan kuzushi

As uke steps forwards to grab tori's wrist, tori turns his palm to face right. As the grip comes on, tori reverses the twist, which has the effect of cutting into uke's grasp and forcing his arm to curl under the grip. tori steps down the gripping side of uke and, as above,

pushes the wrist down and turns his hips to propel uke forwards.

1. ko ho ryote dori
(a) omote waza
(b) ura waza

ko ho ryote dori chudan/gedan kuzushi – omote

uke grabs tori's leading arm and steps down his side to grab the other wrist from behind him. As uke grabs the first wrist, tori turns so that he is parallel with uke when he has stepped down the side for the other wrist. In this position tori pins both wrists to his sides (waki shimete) and steps forwards and across himself in a triangular fashion, so that his front foot is now in line with and in front of the other foot. This will have the effect of twisting uke around tori's torso. tori now breaks the back wrist out of the grip using ri datsu ho and raises the other tegatana hand towards the back of uke's head. Applying a hip turn at the same time finishes the movement, which causes uke to be forced away from tori.

ko ho ryote dori chudan/gedan kuzushi – ura

uke grabs tori as above. As the grab for the leading hand comes on, tori remains facing forwards and brings his hand into his centre, drawing uke slightly on to him. He then raises the tegatana hand through sei chu sen (central line) as for a sword cut. When the tegatana hand is directly above tori's head, he turns to face the other way and cuts the arm downwards in an arc. This breaks uke's balance forwards and downwards. As uke comes up, the other hand raises, palm uppermost, to pick uke up and is then twisted away so that uke falls off the extended arm. tori moves his body through uke's shoulder line to throw him off.

With all of the hachi hon no kuzushi, tori instigates movement in the wrist and body just before the wrist is gripped. This is the principle of go no sen no kuzushi. This allows tori to maximize the use of torque and inertia.

This practice concludes the ki hon ko zo, the building blocks for all aikido technique.

hontai no tsukuri (Creating Opportunity from a Natural Posture)

Physical attacks can be categorized as armed and unarmed. Types of armed attacks are heavily influenced by the weapon being used. However, unarmed attacks can take many forms. Professor Tomiki categorized these into attacks from distance apart (blows and kicks), and attacks involving holding. He developed two forms of technique to combat these types of attack. They are *kansetsu waza*, or joint manipulation techniques, and *atemi waza*, striking techniques. In order to be able to apply these techniques, it is necessary first to 'create' an opportunity. This is called *tsukuri*. tsukuri is a combination of te and tai sabaki, or hand and foot co-ordination. It is also movement into technique.

Below are the basic possibilities for etsu waza no tsukuri.

hontai no tsukuri no kansetsu waza

Holding attacks can be subdivided into aigamae katate dori, or same wrist grab, and gyakugamae katate dori, opposite wrist grab. The defender can break and take grip at jodan or gedan level using a normal grip, junte dori, or a reverse grip, gyakute dori.

Fig 154 aigamae katate dori.

Fig 155 gyakugamae katate dori.

The jodan grips stem from aigamae/gyakugamae chudan kuzushi (see kuzushi, page 94) and can be taken with a junte dori grip or gyakute dori grip.

The gedan grips stem from gedan kuzushi (see kuzushi, page 95) and can be taken with a junte dori or gyakute dori grip.

In total, there are eight possible grips, four from jodan and four from gedan kuzushi. They will determine how the attacker's balance can most effectively be broken – high or low. kansetsu waza no hontai no tsukuri is a grading requirement for 5th to 2nd kyu (see syllabus, pages 166–7). It is practised by uke holding a tanto in one hand and grabbing first aigamae, or same hand, and second gyakugamae, or opposite hand, with a junte dori grip. uke then steps forwards to strike high or low. tori avoids the jodan or gedan strike while taking junte or gyakute dori grips and breaks balance high or low, accordingly.

Fig 156 jodan junte dori.

Fig 157 jodan gyakute dori.

Fig 158 jodan junte dori.

Fig 159 jodan gyakute dori.

Fig 160 gedan aigamae katate dori.

Fig 161 gedan gyakugamae katate dori.

Fig 162 gedan junte dori.

Fig 163 gedan gyakute dori.

Fig 164 gedan junte dori.

Fig 165 gedan gyakute dori.

Once balance is broken there are a number of techniques available to suit that particular outcome. In the grading requirement players are expected to perform oshi taoshi and hiki taoshi from jodan kuzushi and kote gaeshi and tenkai kote gaeshi from gedan kuzushi.

These grips and ways to break balance are tested in the shodokan grading syllabus in isolation, so that only one hand is used. This enables the practitioner to learn how both sides of his body work, before combining the moves to create two-handed grips, with double the power. If the free hand is placed with the gripping hand, this is basically putting the two junte dori or gyakute dori grips together, either at jodan or gedan level, to form a circular grip. The same grips and balance breakers can then be applied to attacks from distance apart, in a tanto bout, or against punches and strikes. These four circular grips lead into the exercise hiji mochi no kuzushi, which is a requirement for 1st kyu examination. Again, this demonstrates Tomiki's progressive system of practice, from single grips taken from a holding attack to circular grips against strikes.

hontai no tsukuri no atemi waza

Players need also to be able to enter into a striking attack that does not employ a grip. The practice for this is commonly known as *uchikomi*, which translates as 'to enter abruptly'. While for stability the aim is to reduce the risk of overbalancing, to initiate movement it is possible to develop a thrust that deliberately leads to overbalancing, so that a horizontal acceleration in a desired direction can be obtained from the interaction with gravity. This principle is essentially what occurs in uchikomi. There are many ways to practise uchikomi but the most basic format is a grading requirement and should be practised as often as possible. The exercise builds up the ability to cross distance at speed, arriving on good posture, and creating

Fig 166 shomen ate preparation.

opportunity for technique. The exercise is applicable to all five of the atemi waza in the randori no kata (*see* page 129).

shomen ate – front strike
Players stand aikido distance apart, and uke stands with feet apart. tori starts from a neutral posture, lowering the posture at the knees.

As tori feels he is falling forwards from the hips, he drives from the left or right foot and arrives with one foot forwards, one back, heels down and the hips and shoulders square (*see* shizentai, page 42). One hand is raised so that tegatana is placed just in front of the face. It is essential that tori initiates the movement with the foot and arm with which he is going to apply technique. In other words, there is only one movement from neutral to tsukuri, creating technique. This greatly reduces the amount of time uke has to avoid or block the move.

Fig 167 Arrival.

Fig 168 shomen ate.

Fig 169 aigamae ate preparation.

As competence grows, the distance between the players and the speed of movement can be increased. Generally, uchikomi stops at the point of arrival, but, after a specified number of entries, tori may throw uke (in this instance, straight backwards) (*see* ukemi, page 65).

On the throw, the posture is lowered as for sho tei awase, and the leading leg moves directly between uke's legs. The head is not forced upwards, but back and downwards. At the point where the hand leaves the head, the forearm (which constitutes part of tegatana) continues contact with uke's chest, until he is forced to take ukemi.

aigamae ate – same-posture strike
tori stands slightly to the side of, and at a slight angle to uke. Uke stands with his feet together.

Fig 170 Arrival.

Fig 171 aigamae ate.

From this position, tori moves in the same way as for shomen ate but the leading foot arrives just to the outside of uke's nearest foot. On the throw, tori brings his arm into centre, which causes uke's head to be tilted to one side, curving his body. The leading foot travels down uke's side. The hips of both players should be touching at the point of throw.

gyakugamae ate – mirror-image posture strike

This exercise starts the same way as ai gamae ate, but tori rotates the hips and lowers the posture to wind up like a spring. The body is then unwound as the back leg drives down uke's side, and the arm is arced up and down to uke's chest.

The chest should not be struck, as the player is attempting to enter at speed in a

Fig 172 gyakugamae ate preparation.

Fig 173 Arrival.

Fig 174 gyakugamae ate.

Fig 175 gedan ate arrival.

Fig 176 gedan ate.

controlled manner. On the throw, tori centres the arm and turns the hips forwards, which twists uke's posture. tori then moves forwards to throw. There should be no gap between tori and uke at the point of throw.

gedan ate – low-level strike
Starting as above, tori winds up the hips and, as the back leg drives down uke's side, tori remains low, creating an oval shape with the arms.

It is important that tori's hips are at least lower than uke's. On the throw, the hips are turned forwards and the leading hip pushes against uke's leading leg. As with aigamae ate and gyakugamae ate, the hips initiate the actual throw. Therefore, it is a bad habit to attempt to grasp uke's legs with the hands and try to lift him. gedan ate can be executed without using the arms at all.

Fig 177 ushiro ate preparation.

Fig 178 Entry.

Fig 179 Arrival.

Fig 180 ushiro ate.

Fig 181 Final position.

ushiro ate – strike from behind

For this exercise, uke stands with feet apart, while tori stands to the side of uke and faces in the opposite direction.

The foot nearest uke moves forwards towards him and is placed just behind him. At the same time, the arms are lifted up and reach behind uke. The leading arm is placed long over uke's shoulder, and the far arm is placed short over the far shoulder.

As tori pivots on the front foot, the short arm pushes the shoulder back, twisting uke's posture. tori then moves back on a 45-degree angle, keeping the same foot forwards, dragging the other shoulder backwards with the long arm. uke is thrown backwards and down as tori moves across him to clear a space for the throw. tori should end with his arms out to his side.

These uchikomi can also be practised while uke stride jumps. This exercise is called sho ki no tsukuri, or 'to seize victory'. In this instance, tori should arrive as uke's legs are apart for shomen ate, closed for aigamae ate, gyakuga-mae ate and gedan ate, and apart for ushiro ate. This will help players with their timing, but also aid their ability to enter with an appropriate technique as uke's posture changes.

The speed at which a player can move and the distance he can cover while arriving on good posture will determine the effectiveness of his technique in randori and renzoku practice (*see* page 153). tsukuri is a fundamental building block for aikido technique. It is best developed through uchikomi, which has many benefits, including the strengthening of the leg muscles and feet, the encouragement of correct posture, an increased knowledge of timing and distance, and the development of an ability to move smoothly across the floor. All competitive forms of budo use some form of uchikomi. As repetitive practices, they are often regarded as tedious or boring, but they bring great rewards in the long run. They are an essential part of training.

Fig 182 Ready to strike.

Four Opportunities to Create Technique

The four elements present in every aikido technique are *tai sabaki*, or avoidance; *irimi*, or entering in; *tsukuri*, or creating opportunity; and *kuzushi*, or balance breaking. *kake*, the technique itself, is the last element to be applied. Even the most direct techniques demonstrate these elements.

All physical attacks from distance apart have the following four elements to them:

- preparation to strike (generally lowering of posture and taking a stance);
- the movement of the attack (arm coming out, leg coming up, body moving forwards, etc.);
- the arrival (focal point of attack); and
- a withdrawal (in preparation to attack again if the first attack was unsuccessful).

Fig 183 Striking.

Fig 184 Arrival at same time.

Fig 185 Avoidance.

Fig 186 Entering in on uke's withdrawal.

Fig 187 Striking.

Fig 188 Smothering strike.

Fig 189 Applying aigamae ate.

Fig 190 Changing to gyakugamae ate.

There are four timing opportunities in the shodokan system that exploit this fact:

1. First opportunity – where the defender moves in at the same time as an attacker strikes, so that when the attacker has arrived at the end point of his attack the defender has already arrived inside it (*see* go no sen, page 47).
2. Second opportunity – where the attacker has missed the target and is moving back into a neutral stance ready to strike again. It is when he begins to withdraw that the defender follows him back and enters in.
3. Third opportunity – where the attacker is preparing to attack and the defender moves in to smother the attack.
4. Fourth opportunity – where the defender has initiated a defence and the attacker has reacted by altering posture. The defender then attacks the new posture.

In this instance, uke is about to be thrown by aigamae ate and so moves his forward leg back to change his posture. This makes aigamae ate inappropriate and so tori now moves down the other side of uke and attempts gyakugamae ate in response. This action, reaction and new action is essentially randori and is what naturally occurs when two people attempt to overcome one another.

The aikidoka needs to practise all four of these opportunities in order to be able to respond quickly to the aforementioned four elements regarding a physical attack.

形

4 Kata

Categorization of Aikido Technique

Professor Tomiki categorized techniques from the various ju jutsu schools taught to him by Ueshiba and Kano into types of technique. These included *atemi waza*, or striking techniques, *kansetsu waza*, or arm twisting and controlling techniques, and *nage waza*, or throwing techniques.

atemi waza (Striking)

Professor Tomiki first recognized three ways of striking an assailant's posture:

- striking the assailant's neutral posture head on (shomen ate);
- striking his right/left posture with an identical posture (aigamae ate); and
- striking his right/left posture with an opposite posture (gyakugamae ate).

Fig 191 Frontal strike.

Fig 192 Identical posture.

Fig 193 Opposite posture.

Fig 194a aigamae ate.

Fig 194b uke turns out.

Fig 194c Attacking from behind.

Fig 195 gyakugamae ate blocked.

Fig 196 Dropping into gedan ate.

In the case of aigamae ate, Tomiki also saw that often an assailant's posture would be turned so far round as to present tori with his shoulders. In this instance, rather than attacking the head, the shoulders or collar would be pulled backwards.

To prevent the technique of aigamae ate, uke has stepped back with his right leg. It is well known that a person will probably attempt to resist having their balance broken by circular movement by turning in the same direction. As he turns his back towards tori to maintain balance, tori moves behind and attacks his new position. This becomes ushiro ate, or strike from behind.

Tomiki also found that if the entry for gyakugamae ate was blocked by the arms, the same entry could also be used to come in low and strike the posture below the hips. This he called gedan ate, or low-level strike.

These five striking techniques comprise the atemi waza and demonstrate the five ways to attack a person's posture with a strike.

There are of course many ways of striking, but Professor Tomiki was particularly interested in the 'blow/throw' method, which continued the strike into a throw. Consequently, the five atemi waza in the randori no kata demonstrate this principle, and contact is maintained with uke's body up to the point of throw. This format constitutes the tachi waza techniques for 5th kyu examination (see page 166). However, the applications for atemi waza are numerous and can be executed against most types of attack (see oyo waza, page 175).

kansetsu waza (Arm Joint Twisting)

Professor Tomiki categorized arm-twisting techniques into techniques that attacked the elbow (hiji waza) and techniques that attacked the wrist (tekubi waza).

The arm can be gripped with a junte dori or gyakute dori grip, which translate as normal and reverse grip, respectively. Players may move inside or outside an attack and take

Fig 197 jodan junte dori.

Fig 198 jodan gyakute dori.

Fig 199 gedan junte dori.

Fig 200 gedan gyakute dori.

Fig 201 Pushing elbow.

Fig 202 Turning and pulling elbow.

either junte dori or gyakute dori grip, which will dictate whether balance is broken at a high level (jodan), or at a low level (gedan). This gives four options:

1. jodan junte dori;
2. jodan gyakute dori;
3. gedan junte dori; and
4. gedan gyakute dori.

These grips are explained further in hiji mochi no kuzushi (*see* page 160).

Once an arm is gripped, either the elbow or wrist may be attacked.

hiji waza (Elbow Techniques)
hiji waza can be divided into pushing the elbow upwards (oshi taoshi), and twisting and pulling the arm inwards to turn the elbow upwards (hiki taoshi).

During the application of both oshi taoshi and hiki taoshi, if uke should resist, then the direction of the elbow can be reversed,

demonstrating the other two ways the elbow can be manipulated. Professor Tomiki called these ude gaeshi and ude hineri.

Fig 203 ude gaeshi.

Fig 204 ude hineri.

Of course, ude gaeshi and ude hineri can be applied independently, but Professor Tomiki placed the four techniques together in the randori no kata because they best demonstrated continuous application of technique for randori practice. Originally, Tomiki classified only four techniques in the hiji waza but he later added waki gatame to represent the way to fix the elbow in a hold. waki gatame literally means 'to harden the armpit', and describes a situation in which the arms are closed into the body to fix the upward position of uke's elbow. waki gatame can be applied after the elbow is raised by pushing or turning and pulling. In other words, waki gatame can be used to lock the arm at the end of oshi taoshi or hiki taoshi.

waki gatame can also be applied independently. Here, too, Tomiki was aware of the possibility to continue from one technique into another, as the responses of uke dictated.

For that reason, both forms are demonstrated in the 4th kyu examination syllabus

(Left) Fig 205 waki gatame ura.

Fig 206 waki gatame omote.

Fig 207 Avoidance.

Fig 208 kuzushi.

for hiji waza techniques. However, only one is demonstrated in the randori no kata. This is because when the tanto is introduced into the randori no kata the strike is avoided to the outside and uke is pulled forwards and diagonally off balance to apply waki gatame.

As with the atemi waza, there are many applications for hiji waza, but they all stem from the elbow being turned upwards or utilize the natural bend at the elbow.

tekubi waza (Wrist Techniques)
tekubi waza techniques attack the wrist. There are two ways to twist the wrist, inwards (kote hineri) and outwards (kote gaeshi).

The wrist can be held and twisted in either direction by the left or right hand, which can be thumb uppermost or turned down.

There are four possible variations of kote hineri:

Fig 209 waki gatame.

Fig 210 kote hineri.

Fig 211 kote gaeshi.

Fig 212 aigamae junte dori kote hineri.

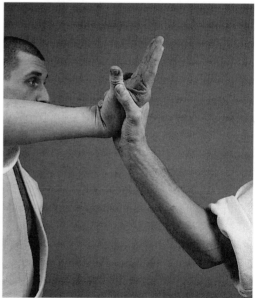

Fig 213 aigamae gyakute dori kote hineri.

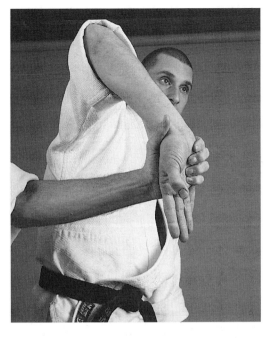

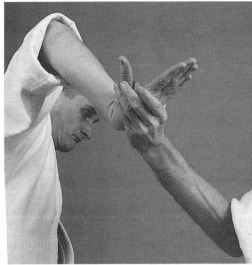

(Left) Fig 214 gyakugame junte dori kote hineri.

Fig 215 gyakugamae gyakute dori kote hineri.

1. aigamae junte dori kote hineri;
2. aigamae gyakute dori kote hineri;
3. gyakugame junte dori kote hineri;
4. gyakugamae gyakute dori kote hineri.

There are four possible variations of kote gaeshi:

1. aigamae junte dori kote gaeshi;
2. aigamae gyakute dori kote gaeshi;
3. gyakugamae junte dori kote gaeshi;
4. gyakugamae gyakute dori kote gaeshi.

In all, there are eight possible tekubi waza grip applications.

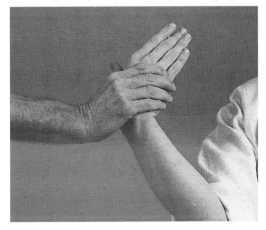

Fig 216 aigamae junte dori kote gaeshi.

Fig 217 aigamae gyakute dori kote gaeshi.

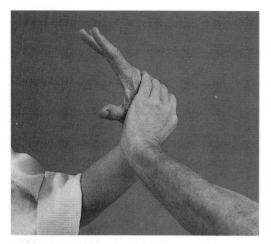

Fig 218 gyakugamae junte dori kote gaeshi.

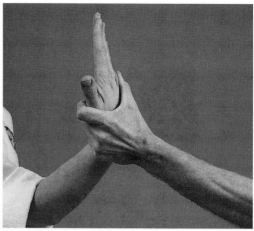

Fig 219 gyakugamae gyakute dori kote gaeshi.

It is possible to take either a junte dori grip or a gyakute dori grip on the wrist with either the left or right hand, and the other hand can be added to strengthen the overall grip. There are two variations. In the first, both thumbs are placed together on the back of the hand. In Fig 220, both hands have taken a gyakute dori grip.

In the second, the thumb is placed alongside the index finger of the other hand. In Fig 221, both hands have taken junte dori grips.

These tekubi waza grips can be applied to any number of different types of attack but will always result in some form of kote hineri, tenkai kote hineri, kote gaeshi or tenkai kote gaeshi. tenkai is employed in techniques where tori has turned through 180 degrees (*see* page 70).

These eight techniques added to the five atemi waza and six hiji waza complete the 19 techniques that Professor Tomiki described as illustrating the possible ways the body's

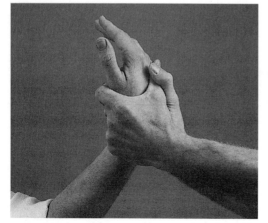

Fig 220 gyakute dori.

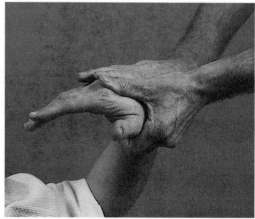

Fig 221 junte dori.

posture may be attacked at a single anatomical point.

The randori no kata demonstrates only four of the possible eight tekubi waza applications. The two basic forms of wrist twisting – inwards for kote hineri, and outwards for kote gaeshi – are shown first. Subsequently, the same techiques are performed with a tenkai turning movement, becoming tenkai kote hineri and tenkai kote gaeshi. These four techniques constitute the tachi waza for 3rd kyu examination.

uki waza (Floating Techniques)

The *uki waza* techniques (*see* i do ryoku, page 175) are those that lift uke up on to the toes in order to effect a throw. *uki* is the infinitive of the Japanese verb *uku*, which means 'to float', or 'feel bouyant'. However, these techniques, following the principles of aikido, only attack one anatomical point. tori is required to move his whole body in a single direction away from, or into one anatomical point, which will cause a dramatic break in uke's balance that is sufficient to lift uke off the floor. This skill is called *i do ryoku*, or the power of body movement.

uchikomi (*see* page 101) is the best exercise to develop this power, since uchikomi develops the ability to move the whole body through distance and at speed while maintaining good posture. The uki waza techniques are not listed in Tomiki's 19 basic techniques because on closer inspection they can be seen to be based on techniques already in the 19.

mae otoshi means 'to fall forwards'. It is no coincidence that mae otoshi follows tenkai kote gaeshi in the ki hon kata. The initial tai sabaki and kuzushi are the same. It is at the point of kuzushi that tori uses body movement against the arm to propel uke forwards; so, mae otoshi is a kote gaeshi with i do ryoku.

sumi otoshi means 'to fall towards the back corner' and is characterized by catching uke's

> ### What is Technique?
>
> It should be understood that the term 'technique' is used loosely in this context, to mean the essential element (goku i) of a technique, which can be applied to a whole range of scenarios (oyo waza, *see* page 175). In other words, why learn 20 techniques, when one technique can be applied to 20 different situations? Using this principle, Professor Tomiki was able to contract the 2,000 or so aikido techniques into 19. This was not to limit the number of techniques available, but to give a better understanding of the quintessential nature of all aikido technique.

wrist at the moment his forward foot touches the ground. In other words, kuzushi occurs at the point just before uke commits all his weight on his front leg. uke's arm is then circled to the side and upwards, as it would be to apply kote hineri. sumi otoshi is a form of kote hineri with i do ryoku.

hiki otoshi means 'to be pulled and fall', and is applied to uke's arm when he continues his movement forwards. This is why an extra step is taken by uke in the randori no kata application of hiki otoshi and uke's balance is broken forwards before technique in hiki otoshi oyo waza. The wrist is turned outwards and is a form of kote gaeshi with i do ryoku.

These three techniques, which Professor Tomiki introduced into free practice and therefore into the randori no kata, comprise the three directions possible to effect uki waza holding the wrist. They appear in the following order:

1. mae otoshi;
2. sumi otoshi; and
3. hiki otoshi.

They direct i do ryoku through a single point (to itsu ryoku, *see* page 176) using forward and backward motion. Again, while Figs 222, 223 and 225 show the three techniques

Fig 222 mae otoshi.

Fig 223 sumi otoshi.

Technical Revision

Through constant observation and revision of techniques, a number of changes are introduced to the sport from time to time, the overriding factor being the safety of both players.

In the case of mae otoshi, it was found that heated exchanges in randori shiai led to many elbows being severely twisted and strained. Therefore, the technique is now only applied with the outside leg driving forwards and uke is restrained rather than thrown forwards. This affords uke a greater opportunity to escape the pressure directed against the elbow.

Fig 224 mae otoshi with outside leg.

as they are commonly seen in the randori no kata, many applications are possible.

These three techniques make up the tachi waza for 2nd kyu examination and conclude the randori no kata.

suwari waza
(Kneeling Techniques)

The Japanese traditionally sat in sei za on tatami mats rather than on chairs and many

Fig 225 hiki otoshi.

Japanese still sit in this way. It was therefore necessary to be able to attack, or to fend off an attack, from this starting position. The vital ability to move swiftly on the knees was called shikko (*see* page 70).

Professor Tomiki developed two sets of techniques: one in which the attacker is standing (hanza handachi), and the other in which both players are seated in sei za (suwari waza). He placed techniques dealing with a variety of attacks from standing and sitting into the goshin no kata or self-defence kata. Tomiki also developed a set of techniques dealing with a standard shomen uchi attack from sitting. This set of eight techniques is called the *suwari waza*; these techniques help to develop timing, kuzushi and arm or wrist pinning. As a learning tool, suwari waza are useful because they are relatively compact in their movement and do not involve large complex movements.

Many aikido techniques place a player on his front, which makes it far harder for the player to continue fighting or struggling, especially if an arm or wrist is pinned. Players may be pinned by someone who remains standing.

In Figs 226 and 227, a kote hineri (inward twist) and a kote gaeshi (outward twist) are

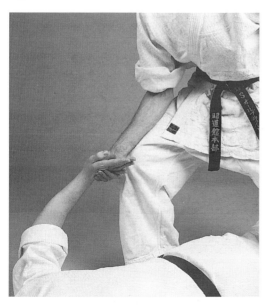

Fig 226 kote hineri osae.

(Right) Fig 227 kote gaeshi osae.

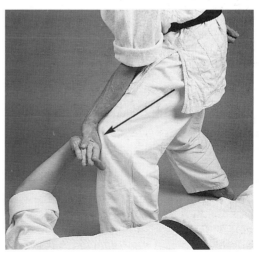

Fig 228 Trapped.

Fig 229 Toes under.

Fig 230 To standing.

Another alternative is to come to the ground with the other player to effect a pin on the ground. These pins are the domain of suwari waza.

When either player moves from sei za to attack or defend, the toes are brought under, to enable a quick rise to standing, if necessary. In Fig 228, the person sitting has failed to come up on to his toes and has become trapped. Figs 229 and 230 show that the player who gets up on to his toes is able to stand up.

In suwari waza, as uke raises his arm in attack, tori mirrors the ascending movement and, at the same instant, moves inside or outside the line of attack. By taking uke's arm with him, tori effects a balance break. In Fig 232, tori has avoided inside; in Fig 233, tori has avoided outside.

From this position, uke's attack should be nullified and he should be unable to attack with the other arm. When it is applied with force, the inside throw requires a falling leaf breakfall from uke (see ukemi, page 63).

applied to the wrist. tori's forearm runs along his thigh and pressure is applied to uke's arm by lowering the knee so that the lock is not applied by just the arm but by the whole body.

Fig 231 Meeting attack.

Fig 232 omote – tori has avoided inside.

Fig 233 ura – tori has avoided outside.

(Right) Fig 234 Falling leaf.

The first two techniques are the most important to master since they require skill in timing, kuzushi, and movement inside or outside the attack. All the other techniques employ these skills but utilize a range of different finishes. These finishes are:

1. oshi taoshi ude hishigi osae;
2. tentai oshi taoshi ude hishigi osae;
3. oshi taoshi gyakute dori kote hineri osae;
4. tentai oshi taoshi gyakute dori kote hineri ude hineri osae;
5. oshi taoshi junte dori kote hineri osae;

6. tentai oshi taoshi junte dori kote hineri ude hineri osae;
7. oshi taoshi tekubi osae;
8. tentai oshi taoshi tekubi osae.

The pin in Fig 239 involves tori extending uke's arm by placing one knee in his ribs and the other inside the thumb of his gripping hand. The knees now push outwards,

Fig 235 ude hishigi osae, omote and ura.

Fig 236 oshi taoshi gyakute dori kote hineri osae, omote.

Fig 237 tentai oshi taoshi gyakute dori kote hineri ude hineri osae, ura.

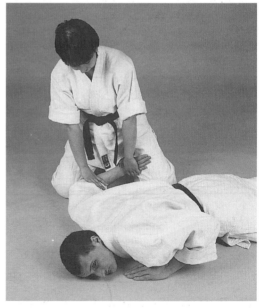

Fig 238 oshi taoshi junte dori kote hineri osae, omote.

Fig 239 tentai oshi taoshi junte dori kote hineri ude hineri osae, ura.

Fig 240 oshi taoshi tekubi osae, omote and ura.

spreading the arm. This opens the elbow joint and the free hand cups the joint and applies downward pressure. This should make it extremely difficult for uke to rescue his arm or move his body. tori pushes his tanden forwards and down so that his centre is very low to the ground and his body weight is evenly distributed above the pin.

As is clear from the names of the techniques, many of the finishes utilize basic wrist twists or combinations of wrist and elbow twists (*see* pages 118–20). osae means 'to pin'.

The second and third pairs of techniques use joint twisting to pin the player to the floor. The first and last pair use two other methods. The first pair use ude hishigi, which means 'to crush the arm', in this instance, applying pressure to the elbow joint. The last pair use tekubi osae, which means 'to pin the wrist'. This is done by placing the first knuckle of the index finger on to the wrist in such a way as to separate the muscles and attack the nerves just above the wrist joint.

The discomfort caused prevents the player from continuing to struggle. The practice to perfect this method of control is called *kime no renshu*. There are several forms of kime in aikido, which attack the nerves.

suwari waza are a grading requirement for 5th to 2nd kyu (*see* pages 166–7).

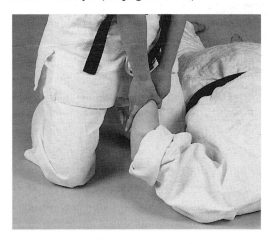

Fig 241 Close-up of kime.

nage no kata
(Throwing Techniques)

nage means 'to throw' and the *nage no kata* is therefore a kata consisting of techniques that throw the attacker away or to the ground. It is the only kata in the shodokan system that deals solely with throws and is an essential learning tool for kuzushi and ju. Done at speed, the kata is dynamic and graceful and epitomizes the throwing art of aikido.

The kata progresses in complexity through 25 techniques. Of these 25 techniques, the first 14 are the most essential to practise, because they are basic moves and can be applied to a number of different scenarios. Of the 14, the first seven are more accurately co-ordinated movements of hands and feet, which effect balance breaks, rather than techniques in their own right. This makes them essential learning tools for understanding the principle of kuzushi.

tori must work out, using the skills developed in the ki hon ko zo, how uke's balance may be broken from aigamae katate dori, gyakugamae katate dori and ko ho ryote dori.

uke is required to feel the direction in which his balance is being broken and respond by moving in that direction and taking ukemi. In this way, uke learns the principle of ju (*see* page 43).

The first six omote, or 'forward of the attack', techniques demonstrate how balance is broken through high, middle and low levels (*see* kuzushi, page 93), and uke is thrown forwards off balance. The seventh, from ko ho ryote dori attack, demonstrates turning forward of the attack (*see* go no sen no kuzushi, page 96).

The first seven moves in the nage no kata are demonstrated for 3rd kyu grading examination and are the first seven balance breakers practised in the hachi hon no kuzushi in the ki hon ko zo (*see* page 93), but uke takes ukemi. The first two moves differ only in that

tori drops to one knee to move uke towards the floor and into zempo kaiten ukemi.

The second group of seven techniques are ura, or 'behind the attack', techniques and take the balance breaks into atemi or kansetsu techniques. The first six ura techniques demonstrate how uke's balance can continue to be broken by moving behind the attack. After initiating high, middle and low balance breaks, they are taken into technique. The last move, again from ko ho ryote dori attack, demonstrates turning behind the attack and is the same as the eighth balance break in the hachi hon no kuzushi in the ki hon ko zo (*see* page 93).

The next section of the nage no kata comprises eight techniques in response to four pairs of grips, and throw uke from omote, in front, or ura, behind, alternately. The last three techniques continue uke's movement in the same direction.

The last 11 techniques are not practised as part of the ki hon ko zo or kyu grading syllabuses but make up the complete nage no kata. The complete kata of 25 techniques is a requirement of 1st, 2nd and 3rd dan for those members who are exempted from the randori free play requirement of those grades.

Because the hachi hon no kuzushi are the most essential eight moves that can be used to generate a balance break, the shihan division has developed a kata that applies them to techniques. This kata is called hachi hon no kuzushi no oyo waza, or applied techniques from eight ways to break balance.

The kata demonstrates the three principles of shizentai, ju and kuzushi as they apply to high, middle and low balance breaking, and atemi waza, hiji waza and tekubi waza are applied respectively. The last pair of ko ho ryote dori grips are dealt with by turning outwards and applying oshi taoshi, and by turning inwards and applying ushiro ate. In this kata, Professor Tomiki's understanding of kuzushi and his quintessential contraction of aikido technique into atemi and kansetsu waza are successfully amalgamated.

The hachi hon no kuzushi oyo waza is part of the requirement for 4th dan.

randori no kata

The randori no kata is also known as ki hon waza or ju nana hon.

Professor Tomiki composed the randori no kata, or set of techniques for free play, by selecting those techniques that could be applied safely and effectively in free play. After many years of practical research, he arrived at the final number of 17 techniques (ju nana hon). This became the most fundamental kata of his system (ki hon waza). The purpose of the kata, as its name suggests, is to introduce players to a set of techniques that lend themselves to a form of continuous practice, *renzoku,* for two individuals.

It is eventually practised as a complete kata as part of the 1st kyu grading syllabus. This is because its component parts are practised in isolation up to this point. At 1st kyu, aikidoka should have a basic grasp of the principles of the 17 techniques and be able to demonstrate the kata in its entirety.

Throughout the kyu grades, up to and including 1st kyu, the kata is practised against a partner who raises an open hand, tegatana, to chest height. tori also raises the same hand to meet uke's (*see* tegatana awase, page 83) and executes techniques from this starting point.

In the early stages, it is useful to gauge correct distance apart, ma ai, by touching the partner's tegatana as in tegatana awase. Later on, tori should attempt to time his technique at the point just before the handblades touch. In this way, tori develops a physical knowledge of a specific distance and timing point for applying technique. The raising of a handblade is not an actual attack but an exercise allowing tori to practise good distance and timing.

In tanto randori and shiai, a match, a tanto is used and the strikes become very fast, so players need gradually to develop the skills in preparation for a fast and committed attack.

The next step in this progressive development is the introduction of the tanto into the kata. The tanto is introduced into the randori no kata at 1st dan, after which the kata is called tanto randori no kata, and it is refined and polished by players through 2nd and 3rd dan. A 3rd dan's timing should be far superior to a 1st dan's, since the tanto randori no kata will have been honed over at least five years' practice! During this time, energetic and youthful players will have applied the skills developed in the practice of this kata in randori practice and shiai competitions.

randori keiko (*see* page 163) is a grading syllabus requirement from 1st through to 3rd dan, for younger players. Older players are required to demonstrate the 25 techniques of the nage no kata instead.

Fig 242 tegatana awase.

Fig 243a Avoidance.

The randori no kata techniques are performed in the following order:

1. atemi waza: shomen ate, aigamae ate, gyakuamae ate, gedan ate, ushiro ate (*see* pages 101–6);
2. hiji waza: oshi taoshi, ude gaeshi, hiki taoshi, ude hineri, waki gatame (*see* pages 115–16);
3. tekubi waza: kote hineri, kote gaeshi, tenkai kote hineri, tenkai kote gaeshi (*see* pages 118–20);
4. uki waza: mae otoshi, sumi otoshi, hiki otoshi (*see* pages 122–3).

For the tanto randori no kata the techniques stay the same, but the timing and distance are altered due to the introduction of a strike. The strike remains straight and at chest height in accordance with the rules dictating striking in shiai competition. There are, however, two technical changes to waki gatame and tenkai kote hineri. The initial avoidance

Fig 243b kuzushi.

Fig 243c waki gatame.

for waki gatame is to the outside of the strike and the arm is not pushed across uke but is taken forwards and diagonally from the strike.

In the case of tenkai kote hineri, the technique is not brought in front of uke but continues backwards away from him.

These technical differences are due to the added dimension of the tanto, because it would be inappropriate for the player to draw the tanto across himself.

ura waza
(Counter Techniques)

The ten techniques in the *ura waza*, or opposing techniques, were developed by Tomiki sensei and Ohba sensei as techniques that most logically countered the techniques of the randori no kata. The purpose of this kata was to demonstrate possible counters to attempted techniques in toshu randori, or free play without a tanto. In the Japanese experience of toshu randori, when two players battled for

Fig 244a Entering in.

Fig 244b tenkai.

Fig 244c kote hineri.

victory, the match would often degenerate into grappling. This is why the tanto was introduced into contests. toshu randori is no longer played in contests in Japan for this reason, but it is demonstrated at formal occasions when all theoretical aspects of Tomiki shihan's system are on display. On such occasions, the two players demonstrate continuous kuzushi and ju – breaking balance for technique and maintaining balance by movement. This continues until a particular balance break is effective to the point of throw, the ultimate expression of kuzushi, at which time a player takes ukemi as the ultimate expression of ju. The nature of true contest does not allow for this co-operative expression.

There are 17 techniques in the randori no kata but only ten techniques in the ura waza. The reason for this is clear upon examination of the 17 techniques.

Of the five atemi waza, shomen ate, gyakugamae ate and gedan ate are open to counters because they are initiated by tori stepping forwards to strike. This creates a timing opportunity, allowing uke to mirror tori's new posture in a way that utilizes the forward momentum of the technique.

Fig 245a shomen ate.

shomen ate countered by waki gatame
As uke steps forwards to strike, tori takes a step back and at the same time lifts uke's striking arm to pull him off posture. uke now has a weak posture forward and to his left. tori exploits this weakness and takes the arm into waki gatame.

aigamae ate countered by oshi taoshi
aigamae ate starts with uke attempting a tentai (partial turn) oshi taoshi and it is at this point that tori counters with oshi taoshi. As uke steps forwards, tori takes a step back and places his hand on top of the hand attacking his elbow. Taking a gyakute dori grip, the hand is raised above uke's head for the balance break leading into oshi taoshi.

Fig 245b Avoidance.

Fig 245c waki gatame.

Fig 246a oshi taoshi kuzushi.

Fig 246b Avoidance.

Fig 246c oshi taoshi.

Fig 247a gyakugamae ate blocked.

Fig 247b Cutting out of grip.

gyakugamae ate countered by gedan ate
uke's attempt at gyakugamae ate is blocked by tori as uke steps forwards. tori takes a step back and slightly to the side, and at the same time twists his hand from uke's grip. He is now in a position to step in under uke's arm for gedan ate.

gedan ate countered by aigamae ate
As uke steps forwards under tori's arm for gedan ate, tori steps back and slightly to the side and brings his forward foot back slightly, too. tori places his arm under uke's and lifts it towards uke's head. At the same time he steps down uke's side for aigamae ate.

ushiro ate countered by tenkai kote hineri
ushiro ate is initiated by uke pushing tori's wrist down to expose the elbow so that he can push it across tori and force his shoulders round. This initial push creates a timing opportunity for tori to move into uke's movement and take the hand for technique.

Fig 247c Entering for gedan ate.

Fig 248a Avoiding gedan ate.

Fig 248b Entering for aigamae ate.

Fig 249a Blocking ushiro ate.

Fig 249b Entry for tenkai kote hineri.

Fig 250a oshi taoshi blocked.

Fig 250b Entry for oshi taoshi.

Fig 251a Pulling arm.

Fig 251b Moving in with pull.

The five hiji waza of the randori no kata consist of oshi taoshi and hiki taoshi, two counters to uke's attempts to protect himself from these, ude gaeshi and ude hineri, and one joint controlling technique, waki gatame, executed on the end of oshi taoshi. Therefore, only the first two techniques, oshi taoshi and hiki taoshi, lend themselves to counter techniques since the other three are already counters to uke's attempts at escape.

oshi taoshi countered by oshi taoshi
As uke takes the forearm and steps back to initiate balance break, tori steps forwards to nullify it. At the same time, he takes gyakute dori grip and pushes the arm up towards uke for a balance break leading to oshi taoshi.

hiki taoshi countered by tenkai kote hineri
uke has attempted hiki taoshi by turning tori's wrist over and is about to pull tori forwards and down. tori does not allow his posture to be broken but uses uke's pull to draw

him in towards uke. As he does this he places his hand on top of uke's so he arrives at uke's side ready to apply tenkai kote hineri.

The next section of the randori no kata is the tekubi waza, and the last three of the four techniques are open to counters at the point of balance break. kote hineri does not have a counter technique since the wrist is immediately twisted and, if applied correctly, cannot be countered other than by pushing the wrist downwards. This defensive action initiates the second technique, kote gaeshi, which is therefore a counter to uke's attempts to escape kote hineri.

Because kote gaeshi is already a response to escaping from kote hineri, and the two techniques are practised in this way in the randori no kata, kote hineri does not appear in the ura waza.

kote gaeshi, tenkai kote hineri and tenkai kote gaeshi are all countered at the point of attempting balance break.

Fig 252 kote hineri.

Fig 253 kuzushi from attempted escape.

Fig 254 kote gaeshi.

kote gaeshi countered by kote gaeshi
uke has attempted kote hineri and tori has countered by pushing his hand downwards (*see above*). uke now takes the hand over into kote gaeshi. tori places his free hand on uke's hand and stops the twist on his own wrist at the point where his fingers are pointing to the ceiling. He then rotates his wrist back the way it came, continuing the movement in a circle. He now has uke's wrist in kote gaeshi and, moving back and across uke to effect a balance break, he applies the technique.

tenkai kote hineri countered by waki gatame
uke has attempted to turn under tori's arm to apply tenkai kote hineri. tori slides his arm up uke's back as he turns and places it between uke's arms. tori then turns and takes uke's arm into waki gatame. In this particular application of waki gatame the elbow is turned over and the thumb of the gripping hand is pinned between tori's tegatana hands.

Fig 255 Attempted kote gaeshi.

Fig 256 kote gaeshi.

Fig 257 Attempted tenkai kote hineri.

Fig 258 waki gatame.

*tenkai kote gaeshi countered by tenkai
kote gaeshi*

uke has attempted to break tori's balance by twisting his arm in. tori has prevented the balance break by placing his arm between uke's and has applied pressure behind uke's elbow (hiji kime) and lowered the tegatana of the other hand to apply leverage to uke's arm. This lifts uke off posture. tori now slides the elbow hand down to uke's wrist and as uke lowers her posture he turns down the side of uke to apply tenkai kote gaeshi.

The last three techniques of the randori no kata, uki waza, are variations of kote gaeshi and kote hineri, with the added impetus of i do ryoku. Since these tenkai kote gaeshi and tenkai kote hineri have already been countered at point of balance break, they are not repeated in the ura waza. For this reason there are only ten ura waza.

Fig 259 Blocking tenkai kote gaeshi.

Fig 260 tenkai ura.

Fig 261 tenkai kote gaeshi.

kaeshi waza
(atemi Counter Techniques)

The *kaeshi waza* were developed by the shi-han technical division of the Japan Aikido Association as a necessary and important development in competitive free play. Aikido was one of the few martial arts in which it was not possible for the person receiving techniques to counter with his own. This was a technical problem borne out of the need to equip uke with enough incentives to attack with conviction during a bout.

Before kaeshi waza, uke was rewarded only with tanto tsukiari, a clear strike to toshu's body with the tanto. However, a tanto strike could only be awarded a single point since the tsukiari is a punitive measure rather than a reward. Therefore, it transpired in practice that the uke who struck at toshu with conviction opened himself up to being thrown, while the uke who played defensively and

negatively was much harder to throw. uke often chose the latter tactic and the play became excessively defensive.

kaeshi waza offers a new incentive for uke to commit his attacks because, for the first time, if toshu attempts to throw him, uke can counter with his own technique.

In the development of kaeshi waza it was necessary to limit the type of techniques that uke could apply from the 17 randori no kata. Since uke was holding on to a tanto, it was obvious that gripping techniques, or kansetsu waza, could not be applied with any degree of effectiveness or safety. If the tanto was dropped, the bout would become toshu randori, which had already been seen to be inappropriate in contest. For this reason, anyone dropping the tanto during a bout is penalized. Since gripping techniques could not be applied, the technical division looked instead at the five atemi waza striking techniques, which could be applied safely and effectively.

Fig 262 shomen ate with empty hand.

Fig 263 gyakugamae ate with tanto hand.

In order to promote play – tanto attempting to strike and toshu encouraged to attempt technique – uke was permitted to initiate a technique only when toshu had two hands on either one of uke's arms.

With his empty hand grabbed, uke would not be able to execute an atemi waza with the other hand that held the tanto without punching, since the hand would be closed around the tanto in a fist. However, if toshu were to grab uke's tanto arm, an atemi waza could be applied safely with that arm, since toshu's own hands would be between him and the technique.

uke is therefore restricted to use of the following atemi waza:

1. toshu grabs uke's tanto arm – uke can apply atemi waza with either arm;
2. toshu grabs uke's free arm – uke can apply atemi waza with that arm only.

Fig 264 Throw with tanto hand.

Fig 265 Throw with open hand.

Fig 266 Throw with gripped open hand.

Seven kaeshi waza with tanto hand

Fig 267 Attempting oshi taoshi.

Fig 268 Countered with ushiro ate.

Fig 269 Attempting hiki taoshi.

Fig 270 Countered with shomen ate.

kaeshi waza has greatly improved aikido play, since both players need constantly to consider the strength and stability of their posture in defence and attack, and both are looking for opportunities to apply aikido technique.

The following is a kata of 14 kaeshi waza techniques that may be used in randori. The kata is by no means exhaustive and was designed by the shihan division of the JAA to demonstrate examples to international aikido teams. Players are encouraged to experiment with logical counters to attempts at aikido techniques, while abiding by the aforementioned restrictions.

atemi waza using the tanto arm: oshi taoshi – ushiro ate
tori is attempting to move down tanto's side to apply a jodan junte dori kuzushi leading to oshi taoshi (*see* Fig 267). tanto moves around the back of toshu and applies ushiro ate.

hiki taoshi – shomen ate
toshu has attempted to twist tanto's wrist over for hiki taoshi. tanto drops the elbow and lowers her posture to prevent balance break and then steps forwards to apply shomen ate.

waki gatame – gyakugamae ate
toshu has attempted to push tanto's arm up for jodan gyakute dori kuzushi leading to waki gatame. tanto drops her elbow and pushes her arm across toshu for gyakugamae ate.

kote gaeshi – ushiro ate
toshu has attempted kote gaeshi. tanto twists her wrist back inside towards her belt knot and at the same time moves around behind toshu for ushiro ate.

tenkai kote hineri – ushiro ate
toshu has attempted to get under tanto's arm to apply tenkai kote hineri. tanto first prevents

Fig 271 Attempting waki gatame.

Fig 272 Countered with gyakugamae ate.

Fig 273 Attempting kote gaeshi.

Fig 274 Countered with ushiro ate.

Fig 275 Attempting tenkai kote hineri.

Fig 276 Countered with ushiro ate.

Fig 277 Attempting tenkai kote gaeshi.

Fig 278 Countered with gyakugamae ate.

Fig 279 Attempting mae otoshi.

Fig 280 Countered with gedan ate.

Seven kaeshi waza with open hand

Fig 281 Attempting oshi taoshi.

Fig 282 Countered with shomen ate.

toshu from getting under the arm by pushing the arm down and at the same time moves around behind toshu for ushiro ate.

tenkai kote gaeshi – gyakugamae ate
toshu has attempted to break tanto's balance for tenkai kote gaeshi. tanto twists her arm round so the elbow is turned upwards and raises the arm to throw with gyakugamae ate.

mae otoshi – gedan ate
toshu has attempted to apply mae otoshi. tanto turns her elbow upwards and pushes her hand down and across toshu. As toshu steps through, tanto applies gedan ate.

atemi waza using the free arm: oshi taoshi – shomen ate
tori is attempting to move down tanto's side to apply a jodan junte dori kuzushi leading to oshi taoshi (see Fig 281). tanto turns to face toshu and applies shomen ate with the free hand. The foot on the same side as the hand must be forward.

hiki taoshi – gyakugamae ate
toshu has attempted hiki taoshi. tanto drops her weight and twists her wrist straight. tanto then steps forwards with the back leg and applies gyakugamae ate with the free hand.

waki gatame – gyakugamae ate
toshu has avoided inside the strike and is lifting the arm up for jodan gyakute dori kuzushi to apply waki gatame. tanto drops her weight and turns her elbow down. tanto then steps in with the back foot and throws with gyakugamae ate with the free hand.

kote gaeshi – gedan ate
toshu has attempted kote gaeshi on tanto's wrist. tanto pushes her elbow up and her wrist down to prevent the technique. tanto now moves under her raised arm to apply gedan ate.

Fig 283 Attempting hiki taoshi.

Fig 284 Countered with gyakugamae ate (front view).

Fig 285 Attempting waki gatame.

Fig 286 Countered with gyakugamae ate (front view).

Fig 287 Attempting kote gaeshi.

Fig 288 Countered by gedan ate (front view).

Fig 289 Attempting tenkai kote hineri.

Fig 290 Countered with ushiro ate.

Fig 291 Attempting tenkai kote gaeshi.

Fig 292 Countered with gyakugamae ate.

Fig 293 Attempting sumi otoshi.

Fig 294 Countered with shomen ate.

tenkai kote hineri – ushiro ate
toshu has attempted tenkai kote hineri. tanto blocks toshu's attempt to get under her arm and moves down the back of her. tanto applies ushiro ate by pulling toshu back with the free hand.

tenkai kote gaeshi – gyakugamae ate
toshu has attempted tenkai kote gaeshi by applying junte dori gedan kuzushi. tanto prevents the balance break by pushing the hand down and turning her elbow up. tanto then steps forwards with the back foot and applies gyakugamae ate with the free hand.

sumi otoshi – shomen ate
toshu has attempted sumi otoshi. Before balance is broken, tanto quickly steps around to face toshu and applies shomen ate.

This concludes the kata. The shihan division is keen to point out that these are not the only

counters a player can perform. For example, a gedan ate may be applied instead of a gyakugamae ate in certain instances. Also, this kata does not demonstrate atemi waza available to tanto if the free hand is gripped. If this is the case, tanto can only use the free hand to apply technique.

For example, in Figs 295 and 296, toshu has grabbed the free hand and tanto has applied gyakugamae ate with that hand. Usually, when toshu grabs the free hand, a player will place the tanto on to toshu's chest, and toshu must attempt to move it. For reasons of safety, tanto is not permitted to strike at such close range. However, if toshu makes no attempt to remove the tanto arm, he will be cautioned with tai sabaki shido, or penalty for non-avoidance.

Players must learn to feel what is right at any given time in randori practice. tanto should avoid preconceiving a kaeshi waza technique before toshu has attempted technique.

Fig 295 Open-hand gripped.

Fig 296 gyakugamae ate with open hand.

Fig 297 tanto on chest.

Fig 298 Moving tanto off chest.

乱取り方

5 Methods of Training for randori

The Purposes of Practice

It can be argued that there is always a perfect moment to apply any technique, whereby there is no effective resistance. This perfect moment, however, cannot be learned in kata or embu alone because it is given; there is no experiential reference. A player may execute a technique twice and be happier with one or the other in technical terms, but may not be able to distinguish one moment over others, since it has been given to him by his collusive partner. In randori, there is an almost infinite number of moments in which a player may attempt a technique, but only very few moments when the technique could be applied without effort. These moments when a technique might be applicable will come and go if tori is too slow to respond, or simply fails to see them. randori allows a player to build up a body of knowledge based on experience, which will help to distinguish the number of moments that are relevant to a finite number of techniques (*see* randori no kata, page 129).

The main problem with randori practice is that participants tend to bypass several essential technical skills. Under stress, players revert to using natural resources such as muscular strength and endurance. They also tend to suffer 'tunnel vision', focusing all their energy and thought on one point, both in attack and defence, regardless of continuing events.

All martial arts are unnatural – they utilize natural energy and physiology in a new way, which has to be learned. Players need to be able to maintain an open mind and posture; they need to be able to see the whole picture, even while under severe duress. This ability can mean the difference between victory and loss in the sports arena, victim or non-victim on the street, and, ultimately, survival or otherwise in a life-threatening scenario. To achieve this openness, players must have basic skills instinctively at their command; the only way to achieve this is through years of practice.

Fighting is incredibly tiring and demanding, both aerobically and anaerobically. Explosive muscular strength utilizes energy stored in the muscles, which is used up after about six to ten seconds. Therefore, it is essential to use that source of strength in an effective manner, and to be in a tactical position before it is used.

Inexperienced martial arts players tend to use an enormous amount of energy aerobically, achieving very little. Once engaged in a bout, they meet strength with strength head on, burning up anaerobic energy sources. More experienced players conserve energy while they seek tactical openings, and use explosive energy only when it is necessary and useful. The difference is even more marked in martial arts bouts that employ weapons, due to the extra respect given to the weapons.

Professor Tomiki introduced the tanto into competitive aikido to ensure that players stayed apart. Unfortunately, since the tanto is made of foam rubber, many players forget

Fig 299 Attempted aigamae ate *(above left)*, continued *(above)* into ushiro ate *(left)*.

avoidance, through a series of progressive levels, to competition. This format ensures that all participants gain long-term benefit. The complexity of randori practice is characterized by the degree of unpredictability in the attacks and defence. The level of unpredictability, from totally predictable to *very* unpredictable, is increased only gradually. ('Totally unpredictable' would characterize a real combat situation and is therefore inappropriate in practice and sport.)

renzoku keiko means 'continuous practice', and allows players to work with a continuous attack and continuous attempts at technique. renzoku keiko presupposes that a single technique is unlikely to be sufficient to throw or control an opponent in a randori context. Players move logically from one failed technique to the next until the other

that it represents a weapon and the martial skills of avoidance are sometimes lost. randori practice must graduate from basic

Fig 300 Attempted gyakugamae ate *(above)* turns into gyakute dori gedan kuzushi *(above right)*, which leads into kote gaeshi *(right)*.

player's balance is broken sufficiently, and they are thrown or pinned. Tomiki sensei categorized atemi striking techniques and kansetsu arm techniques for use in randori and these techniques are interchangeable within their own categories and between the categories.

The possible combinations of techniques are therefore:

- atemi waza to atemi waza (attempted aigamae ate continued into ushiro ate);
- atemi waza to kansetsu waza (attempted gyakugamae ate turns into gyakute dori gedan kuzushi which leads into kote gaeshi);
- kansetsu waza to kansetsu waza (hiki taoshi is resisted and subsequently turned into ude hineri); and
- kansetsu waza to atemi waza (kote gaeshi is resisted by uke who is then open to shomen ate).

Fig 301 hiki taoshi *(above left)* is resisted and subsequently turned into *(above)* ude hineri *(left)*.

Figs 299 and 302 represent examples only of possible combinations. Players are encouraged to experiment with their own choice of

techniques. Once one of these combinations has been attempted, strings of techniques can be tried, according to and dependent on the evasive actions of uke.

Progressive Training in Class

It is only by utilizing progressive systems of practice that players can explore all the elements of randori. Generally, in a class situation, the following progressive training methods are worked through.

tai sabaki

tai sabaki means 'body handling'. In this context, it means the ability to move at speed, from a natural posture, into a kamae, while avoiding an attack. This is closely linked with the

principle of i do ryoku (*see* page 175). There is little point in being able to evade an attack if you do not arrive in a controlled and stable posture from which to apply aikido technique.

tai sabaki practice is not concerned with the use of the hands (tegatana), so it requires a totally predictable and straight attack with the tanto. This attack, however, can be quick or slow, depending on a player's ability to avoid.

At this stage of practice, a high side attack (yokomen and gyakumen) can also be used. Avoidance for straight attacks utilizes the directions in un soku except for straight forwards and back, which are used to avoid side strikes. Avoidance for high attacks is a movement into the slowest part of the attack, which is the armpit of the attacking arm.

tai sabaki is by far the most important randori practice since, if an attack is not avoided, aikido is of little use.

Fig 302 kote gaeshi is resisted by uke *(above)*, who is then open to shomen ate *(below)*.

Fig 303 yokomen uchi.

157

Fig 304 gyakumen uchi.

Fig 305 yokomen uchi.

Fig 306 gyakumen uchi.

tegatana no bogyo

tegatana no bogyo means 'handblade defence'. It is the use of the hands (te sabaki), combined with the movement of the body (tai sabaki), that constitutes effective avoidance. As in tegatana dosa (*see* pages 79–83), there are three levels at which to use tegatana – high, middle and low. For the purposes of randori practice, the majority of strikes are aimed at mid-torso height. This means that the majority of tegatana are placed at middle, or chudan, level. However, high side strikes (yokomen and gyakumen) can also be used in this practice.

The purpose of tegatana, in this instance, is to block the strike at its slowest point, again, as close to the armpit as possible. However, moving into a yokomen strike, the forearm must also be blocked, to prevent the attack bending at the elbow.

Apart from the above-mentioned attacks, the purpose of tegatana no bogyo is not to

Fig 307 Two-handed defence.

Fig 308 Outside corner left arm.

Fig 309 Outside corner right arm.

block an attack, since it is unnecessary to block an attack that has already missed. Its purpose is to create a physical reference point with the attacking limb, so that it is possible to control or 'read' its movement. For this reason, the use of tegatana needs to be soft and responsive, not stiff and slow. tegatana no bogyo does not negate the need for tai sabaki, it is simply the next step.

For avoidance purposes, keeping the hands in sei chu sen alignment, it is helpful to first practise keeping the hands together as for ga sho uke, then one hand can be used. The direction of tai sabaki and the choice of te sabaki determines which grip should be taken and in which direction balance should be broken.

This leads on logically to the next exercise.

Fig 310 Inside corner left arm.

Fig 311 Inside corner right arm.

hiji mochi no kuzushi

This exercise demonstrates the ways to take uke's arm and break his balance. There are two levels at which to break balance while holding on to uke's arm: jodan and gedan, or high and low. A player can avoid inside or outside an attack, and can take a circular grip on the wrist, with his right or left hand on top. Therefore, there are four different opportunities for balance breaking: jodan junte dori; jodan gyakute dori; gedan junte dori; and gedan gyakute dori.

From these four openings, it is possible to perform a number of techniques; for the purposes of the shodokan grading syllabus, oshi taoshi, waki gatame, tenkai kote gaeshi and kote gaeshi are performed.

Note that the thumb is uppermost on the elbow in the application of oshi taoshi in hiji mochi no kuzushi (*see* Fig 312). This is because of the positioning of the hands on uke's arm initially, which ensures that any resistance by pushing the elbow down does not come down on tori's thumb. Also, at the point of balance break, the thumb is in line with its forearm for added strength.

This exercise is an examination requirement for 1st kyu.

kakarigeiko

kakarigeiko means 'light practice'. In the context of randori practice, it provides an opportunity to try out techniques from the randori no kata and to practise taking the falls. tanto strikes straight for the torso and does not withdraw the tanto, allowing toshu to execute techniques. Players can build up their vocabulary of techniques and practise them without worrying about resistance or counter attacks

hiji mochi no kuzushi

Fig 312 jodan junte dori.

Fig 313 jodan gyakute dori.

Fig 314 gedan junte dori.

Fig 315 gedan gyakute dori.

Fig 316 oshi taoshi.

Fig 317 waki gatame.

Fig 318 tenkai kote gaeshi.

Fig 319 kote gaeshi.

162

from uke. kakarigeiko can be practised at all levels of ability.

hikitategeiko

hikitategeiko literally means 'practice which helps tori to advance his ability to defeat uke'. In randori practice, this means that uke does not fall unless tori's technique is effective to the point of balance break. If it is not, uke moves around the attempted technique, and tori has to attempt a new technique relevant to the new situation. This helps tori understand how uke is likely to try and avoid the techniques and to build up a sequence of techniques that logically follow each other. During this practice, uke can also vary the speed and distance of attacks and can also 'feint', to tempt tori to move before a strike. The level of unpredictability of attack should be directly related to the ability of tori.

randori keiko

In free play practice, uke can attack with the tanto at will, within the confines of the rules laid down for the sport, and can use any amount of movement necessary to resist tori's technique. toshu attempts to apply technique, having developed power in the technique through the process of kata, kakarigeiko and hikitategeiko. Through attempting to apply technique, toshu also trains his spirit and body. randori keiko

should always be used as a means of improving the participants' aikido, so both uke and tori should concentrate on good balance and posture, correct distance during play and good tai sabaki. aikido players constantly try to work towards aikido that does not rely on strength. A perfect technique should feel effortless and spontaneous.

randori shiai

Having practised randori keiko, participants can opt to take part in *shiai*, which is a match. randori keiko and randori shiai are not the same thing and people who do not wish to take part in matches should continue to attempt to progress their aikido using the above methods of practice. Those who wish to carry on into competitive aikido may do so at various competitions, held regionally, nationally and internationally, following universally accepted rules.

shiai is a unique opportunity for a player to test his aikido against people with whom he does not normally train and will add to the unpredictability of practice. Players are also afforded the safety that all universal sports must promote. With objective referees to decide victory and loss, bouts rarely result in serious injury. While nobody likes losing, there are always more lessons to be learned in defeat than in victory and players should therefore see all shiai as a 'win/win' situation.

審查內要

6 Grading Syllabus

Belt Systems

The original grading syllabus began at 5th kyu and Professor Tomiki adopted a coloured belt scheme at shodokan hombu dojo in Osaka to differentiate the various kyu grades. The belt is worn around the waist to keep the training jacket closed during training. The 5th, 4th and 3rd kyu are represented by a green belt and 2nd and 1st kyu are represented by a brown belt. In the university clubs in Japan, the coloured belts are not worn, and the traditional system of wearing a white belt until being awarded a black belt is preferred. It is important to note that the black belt is awarded at shodan, which means 'beginner level'.

The coloured belt system was probably a result of the need to protect lower-graded players who were workers and could not, therefore, afford to risk injury, and who paid instructors' wages. Such players could easily identify each others' ability from the belts worn, and would practise accordingly. In the universities, loss of employment is not a primary concern and training is more extensive and vigorous. There are those who shun the coloured belt system as representative of a Western desire for fast results, putting more emphasis on getting the next belt rather than training for its own sake. However, it can also be argued that the award of each coloured belt brings a sense of responsibility to the player to impart his own knowledge, however small, to those of a lower grade.

The black belt was originally a white belt, which became grey after many years of use. At some point it became desirable to obtain a 'black' belt, and the belts are now made of dyed black material. The Japanese colour scheme was devised so that a white belt could be dyed a number of colours over time until finally it was dyed black. Today, there are many coloured belts for sale, catering for a wide range of different martial arts.

The Gradings

After making the decision that the leap from beginner to 5th kyu was too great, the technical division of shodokan aikido introduced 8th, 7th and 6th kyu, to ease the transition. The colour adopted for these grades is light blue. The shodokan division of the British Aikido Association has adopted the following colours for each of the grades:

- 8th; 7th and 6th kyu = red
- 5th kyu = yellow
- 4th kyu = orange
- 3rd kyu = green
- 2nd kyu = blue
- 1st kyu = brown

These colours are used only by children in Japan.

The 8th, 7th and 6th kyu gradings introduce players to fundamental skills that they will need to carry on through the grades. The first requirement is ukemi, or breakfalling, the two basic falls being the backward breakfall and the forward rolling breakfall. These are progressed through the three grades from squatting and kneeling to standing (*see* page 63).

The next requirements are the correct execution of unosku, or foot movements, and tegatana dosa, or handblade moves. These are demonstrated in 8th and 7th kyu respectively. They show a basic understanding of body movement, and body, foot and hand co-ordination (*see* page 78–83).

There are nine techniques that demonstrate the principles of atemi waza, hiji waza and tekubi waza in each grade – in other words, one of each category in each grade. These three categories of technique comprise Professor Tomiki's contracted 19 techniques of aikido. The techniques are all performed from grips so that the beginner does not have to concentrate too hard on correct distance and timing.

8th kyu
- Backward breakfall from squatting
- unsoku (foot movements)

The techniques for 8th kyu are all performed from aigamae katate dori, cross-handed grip.
- aigamae katate dori: shomen ate, oshi taoshi, kote gaeshi.

7th kyu
- Forward breakfall from kneeling
- tegatana dosa (handblade moves)

The techniques for 7th kyu are all performed from gyakugamae katate dori, straight grip.
- gyakugamae katate dori: aigamae ate, hiki taoshi, tenkai kote hineri.

6th kyu
The three techniques for 6th kyu are performed from different attacks. They are:

- ko ho ryote dori – gyakugamae ate
- aigamae katate dori – waki gatame
- han za han dachi gyakugamae katate dori – tenkai kote gaeshi

From 5th kyu to 1st kyu, there are two complete kata. They are demonstrated in sections, so that by 1st kyu they are demonstrated in their entirety. These are randori no kata and suwari waza.

The ura waza is introduced in its entirety at 1st kyu.

The rest of the contents of the kyu grade syllabuses progressively teach core skills to take into the dan grade syllabi.

5th kyu
- randori no kata – atemi waza
  shomen ate
  aigamae ate
  gyakugamae ate
  gedan ate
  ushiro ate
- suwari waza
  oshi taoshi hishigi osae
  tentai oshi taoshi ude hishigi osae
- hontai no tsukuri
  kansetsu waza – jodan – tegatana no tsukuri
  aigamae katate dori – oshi taoshi
  gyakugamae katate dori – hiki taoshi
  atemi waza – uchikomi
  shomen ate
  aigamae ate

4th kyu
- randori no kata – hiji waza
  oshi taoshi
  ude gaeshi
  waki gatame
  hiki taoshi
  ude hineri
  waki gatame

- suwari waza
  oshi taoshi gyakute dori kote hineri osae
  tentai oshi taoshi gyakute dori kote hineri ude hineri osae

- hontai no tsukuri
  kansetsu waza – gedan – tegatana no tsukuri
  tenkai kote gaeshi
  kote gaeshi

- atemi waza – uchikomi
  gyakugamae ate
  gedan ate
  ushiro ate

3rd kyu
- randori no kata – tekubi waza
  kote hineri
  kote gaeshi
  tenkai kote hineri
  tenkai kote gaeshi

- suwari waza
  oshi taoshi junte dori kote hineri osae
  tentai oshi taoshi junte dori kote hineri ude
  hineri osae

- hontai no tsukuri
  kansetsu waza – nigiri kaeshi – jodan no
    kuzushi

    oshi taoshi
    hiki taoshi

  atemi waza – shoki no tsukuri
    shomen ate
    aigamae ate
    nage no kata – omote

2nd kyu
- randori no kata – uki waza
  mae otoshi
  sumi otoshi
  hiki otoshi

- suwari waza
  oshi taoshi tekubi osae
  tentai oshi taoshi tekubi osae

- hontai no tsukuri
  kansetsu waza – nigiri kaeshi – gedan no
    kuzushi
    kote gaeshi
    kote gaeshi

atemi waza – shoki no tsukuri
  gyakugamae ate
  gedan ate
  ushiro ate
  nage no kata – ura

1st kyu
- randori no kata (17)
- ura waza (10)
- hontai no tsukuri
  atemi waza – shoki no tsukuri
    gyakugamae ate
    gedan ate
    ushiro ate
  kansetsu waza – hiji mochi no kuzushi
    jodan junte dori – oshi taoshi
    jodan gyakute dori – waki gatame
    gedan junte dori – tenkai kote gaeshi
    gedan gyakute dori – kote gaeshi
- randori ho
  tai sabaki

This concludes the kyu grade examination syllabuses. Players will have learned the core skills, in particular the randori no kata, in preparation for the next three dan grade levels, which usually span a player's competitive years. Of course, a player may start to learn aikido later in life and will gain many benefits from the shodokan syllabus, which does not include a compulsory competitive element. It is important to remember that randori in itself is not competitive.

goshin no kata

goshin no kata means 'a formal set of self-defence techniques'. There are 50 techniques in the goshin no kata, which make up part of the grading syllabuses from 1st dan black belt to 3rd dan black belt.

The techniques are executed with both players kneeling, the attacker standing, and both players standing for 1st dan; attacks with a tanto for 2nd dan; and attacks with a bokken, attacks with a jo, defence with a jo and bokken against bokken for 3rd dan.

As well as the goshin no kata, the randori no kata is now executed against a tanto attack and becomes the tanto randori no kata, demonstrating an ability to time and execute the techniques from a straight, striking attack. The timing point for all 17 techniques therefore differs from the basic randori no kata format. waki gatame and tenkai kote hineri differ technically, due to slight variations in the weak line of uke's stance. It is repeatedly demonstrated through 1st to 3rd dan.

For those players of more advanced age, the nage no kata is demonstrated in its entirety rather than the usual randori requirement.

1st dan

• tanto randori no kata
• goshin no kata – 16 techniques
  suwari waza – four techniques
  hanza handachi – four techniques
  tachi waza – eight techniques
• randori ho
  kakarigeiko
  hikitategeiko
  (2 mins as tori and uke for each component)

2nd dan

• tanto randori no kata
• goshin no kata first sixteen techniques plus:
  goshin no kata – tanto dori
• randori ho
  tanto randori
  (2 mins as tori and uke × 3)
  Exempted people nage no kata: omote and ura (14 techniques)

3rd dan

• tanto randori no kata
• goshin no kata – first 24 techniques plus:
  bokuto dori – taking sword
  yari dori – taking spear
  yari – jo wins
  kumi tachi – sword versus sword

• randori ho
  tanto randori
  (2 mins as tori and uke × 4)
  Exempted people nage no kata: omote and ura plus oyo waza.

Just as hontai no tsukuri are practice exercises for kansetsu waza and atemi waza, so suburi waza for bokken and jo are practice exercises, which develop such skills as timing, body handling, cutting and power in aikido technique. The suburi waza for the bokken relate directly to the tegatana dosa (*see* page 80).

The traditional schools of aikido teach a 31 jo kata. However, Professor Tomiki and Ohba sensei were conscious that this kata was too long and difficult for contemporary players to master, given the length of time afforded to leisure pursuits. They revised the 31 jo kata to

---

Weapons: bokken and jo

The 3rd dan syllabus represents the first time that the bokken and jo weapons are introduced in examination. Learning to cut with a bokken and handle a jo properly takes many years of practice, so the sooner players begin to handle them, the better. The weapons are not real – they are in fact bits of wood – and the techniques against them are not 'advanced'. Professor Tomiki and Ohba sensei included the use of the jo and bokken because they are excellent tools for developing powerful and graceful aikido technique. Today's aikido player is not a 16th-century samurai warrior, so, for the sake of safe practice, the bokken and jo are no longer replicas of actual weapons but merely learning aids. Other martial arts, such as jodo and iaido, explore more deeply the proper use of a spear or a sword. A kendo master might find many faults in an aikidoka's use of the bokken, from a kendo point of view. From Professor Tomiki's point of view, the use of the jo and the bokken is very much an extension of unarmed aikido technique, and vice versa. For example, the tegatana dosa from the ki hon kozo clearly demonstrate the use of sword cutting movements, but are also prevalent in aikido technique.

Fig 320 jo suburi preparation.

Fig 321 Strike to heart.

Fig 322 Defensive posture.

a basic six jo kata and a 21 jo kata. However, the shihan division of shodokan aikido became aware that even the 21 count jo kata was too complex and difficult. It was further revised to an 18 count jo kata, and this is taught at hombu dojo today.

The six count jo kata
Preparation Position and Manoeuvre 1
To strike towards an opponent's heart, the arms swing backwards, keeping the jo at the same angle. The hand on the butt of the jo stays firm, while the upper hand remains soft and rolls under the jo on its withdrawal. As the player steps forwards off the central line, the jo is brought forwards to the point where the hand on the butt nestles into the hip and the upper hand rolls on to the top of the jo. This makes the strike and the posture strong.

Manoeuvres 2 and 3
From the strike to the heart, the jo is brought up above the head as the player moves backwards and across the central line. The back of the butt hand faces down directly above the head. The upper hand is open, with the jo resting in the crook of the thumb. This is a

Fig 323 Strike to side of head.

Fig 324 Defensive posture.

defensive stance and the jo is angled in such a way as to protect the head and body from a straight cut. The jo is brought forwards by sliding both the butt hand and upper hand together, sliding the open hand over the butt hand and sliding both hands back out, so that the hands have changed places along the jo. During this manoeuvre, the back leg is brought round into a new posture. The tip of the jo is now level with an imaginery opponent's head.

Manoeuvres 4 and 5

From the strike to the head, the jo is allowed to slide through the hands until the tip of the jo is held by the forward hand. During this manoeuvre, the player steps back and across the straight line of attack. From this position, the player steps forwards by bringing the back foot round, and strikes at knee height. The jo is held tightly across the thighs.

Manoeuvre 6

This manoeuvre returns the player to the beginning, ready to start again. Having struck low, the jo is twisted round through 180

Fig 325 Strike to knee.

Fig 326 Preparation for strike to heart.

Fig 327 Powerful movement.

Fig 328 Powerful arrival.

degrees by the forward hand, as the hand at the tip of the jo slides along the whole length to the butt. During this manoeuvre, the player steps back, the forward foot coming up on to the toes and slightly across the line of the back foot ready to step forward again. The player is now ready to repeat the moves again.

These six jo kata can be performed in tandem, with the jo connecting at chudan, jodan and gedan levels respectively. It is also possible to use the same six moves to defend and attack shomen cuts with the bokken. This relates to the six direction avoidance kata.

In the shodokan system of aikido, emphasis is placed upon the power of i do ryoku and the position of the arms and hands in relation to the weapon and the body. For example, no attempt is made to disguise the length of the jo in attack; instead, the power of body and arm movement in attack is developed along similar lines to uchikomi.

In Fig 327, tanto is striking with speed and power, and toshu is responding with a similar movement in defence. Both players are moving in a powerful way, which also corresponds with the movement of the player as he strikes forwards with the jo. There is often one hand open and one hand closed on the weapon at any given time, allowing fluidity of movement, which can also be brought directly into the unarmed techniques and randori practice. The open hand directs and the closed hand controls, whether holding an arm or a bokken.

The six-manoeuvre suburi waza should be practised as much as possible, from beginner level through to 3rd dan and beyond. This ensures good preparation for the 3rd dan examination and, more importantly, a greater understanding of aikido movement and technique.

goshin ho

goshin ho means 'methods of self-defence'. There are 57 techniques in the goshin ho, which make up the grading syllabuses from 4th dan to 7th dan. Each syllabus demonstrates different themes and skills. For example, the 4th dan syllabus explores kuzushi and application techniques from the go no sen timing point. The 5th dan syllabus explores the theme of leading an opponent into a weaker posture before executing technique. The 6th dan syllabus explores a variety of attacks in which the training jacket is grasped in a number of ways. The 7th dan syllabus revisits the 6th dan syllabus and explores applied use of tegatana, datsu ryoku and kaiten. These are just some of the characteristics of the goshin ho which, combined with the complete goshin no kata and tanto randori no kata, constitute the dan level technical syllabuses of Tomiki shihan's shodokan aikido.

4th dan

Players taking the 4th dan exam are also required to demonstrate a section of the buki (or weapons) requirement for 3rd dan. The section is selected by the senior exam panel. In Japan, players also undergo an oral exam and must submit an essay on a selected chapter from Tomiki shihan's book *budoron* (or 'Discussions on budo').

- tegatana no kuzushi no oyo waza (eight techniques)
- goshin ho tekubi dori
  aigamae katate dori
      9 shomen ate
      10 gedan ate

- gyakugamae katate dori
  11 shomen ate
  12 aigamae ate
  13 gyakugamae ate

- goshin ho da totsu shu – techniques against strikes, punches and kicks
  shomen uchi
      14 aigamae ate
      15 oshi taoshi

  yokomen uchi
      16 aigamae ate
      17 tenkai kote gaeshi

  shomen tsuki – punch to solar plexus
      18 kote gaeshi

  mae geri – straight kick to front
      19 shomen ate

5th dan
- goshin ho tekubi dori
  aigamae katate dori
      1 oshi taoshi
      2 hiki taoshi
      3 kote hineri
      4 kote gaeshi
      5 tenkai kote hineri

  gyakugamae katate dori

6 hiki taoshi
7 gyakute dori kote hineri
8 waki gatame
9 tenkai kote gaeshi
10 sumi otoshi

katate ryote dori
11 oshi taoshi
12 kote gaeshi

zempo ryote dori
13 aigamae ate (tenchi nage)
14 aigamae ate (tenchi nage ura)

ko ho ryote dori
15 tenkai ude hineri nage
16 kote gaeshi
17 tenkai kote gaeshi
18 tenkai gyakute dori kote hineri

6th dan
- goshin ho dogi dori – techniques from gi grabbing attacks
mae eri dori – grabbing front collars of gi with one hand
1 gyakute dori kote hineri osae

aigamae naka sode dori – grabbing sleeve at elbow in same posture
2 kote gaeshi

gyakugamac naka sodc dori – grabbing sleeve at elbow in mirror posture
3 waki gatame
4 gyakute dori kote hineri osae

ryo sode dori – grabbing both sleeves
5 gedan ate

ju ji jime – crossed hand strangle using gi collars
6 tenkai kote hineri

okuri eri dori – grabbing collar from behind

7 kote hineri
8 kote gaeshi

kakae dori – bear hug
9 tenkai kote hineri
10 gyakute dori kote hineri

- datsu ryoku – breaking balance without strength (soft arm)
aigamae katate dori
11 aigamae ate

katate ryote dori – two hands grab one hand
12 tenkai kote gaeshi

- tegatana – balance breaking using tegatana handblade
gyakugamae katate dori -
13 ushiro ate
14 kote gaeshi
15 tenkai kote gaeshi

zempo ryote dori – frontal two hand grab
16 hiji kime taoshi
17 gyakute dori kote hineri osae
18 tenkai kote gaeshi

7th dan
6th dan techniques re-visited plus kaiten (balance breaking using a hip turn)
aigamae katate dori
1 aigamac atc (from jodan kuzushi)

ryo naka sode dori
2 ude hineri ude gaeshi (from chudan and gedan kuzushi)

7th dan constitutes the highest examinable grade in the shodokan system. The required length of time between grades necessitates upwards of 30 years of continuous practice, but in reality only a handful of extremely dedicated practitioners could hope to attain this level of proficiency and technical knowledge.

応用技

7 Application Techniques

Part of Professor Tomiki's genius was that he was able to extrapolate from the vast rubric of ju jutsu techniques being practised at the time the fundamental skills that they all employed. There are around 2,000 aikido techniques, but Tomiki managed rationally and logically to reduce them to a set of 19. His reason for doing this was not to restrict aikido participants, but to make the techniques easier to learn. He recognized that a great number of 'techniques' were actually the same technique, applied in a number of different scenarios. There may be slight differences in the attack, or in the way the technique is executed, but the technique is fundamentally the same. Consequently, with a full understanding of the fundamental technique, the player could apply it to any number of situations.

The direction in which the joints of the body can be manipulated is finite. Rather than studying every possible situation that might arise, it is easier to study the limitations of the human anatomy and then learn how to exploit them in any given situation. Once Tomiki had arrived at 19 techniques – the smallest number possible to exploit weakness in posture and the elbow and wrist – all other techniques became *oyo waza*, or application techniques. For example, in aikido practice you might be attacked by any one of shomen/yokomen/gyakumen uchi, tsuki, keri, aigamae/gyakugamae katate dori, morote dori, ko ho ryote dori, dogi dori, and so on, yet all the attacks can be dealt with by a single technique such as gyakugamae ate. In order to do this, you need not only a full understanding of the technique, but also a deep appreciation of the three principles of shizentai, ju and kuzushi. The principles lead to an examination of many other attributes of aikido technique and also to a study of how your own body can be used to best effect, with maximum efficiency and minimum effort. With this aim in mind, Tomiki also researched the way in which a person could utilize his own body in different ways to effect technique in different situations. This led to the study of the skills described below.

i do ryoku (the Power of Movement)

i do ryoku is the power of body movement – the way in which a person can move from a to b, at speed and in posture. If you are pulled and you step forwards at that moment, you are propelled forwards and you can utilize the pull (for example, ki hon no kata ura waza – hiki taoshi countered by tenkai kote hineri). Similarly, if you are pushed you can move backwards with the direction of the push to cause the attacker to fall forwards (for example, ki hon no kata ura waza – shomen ate countered by waki gatame). Of course, you can also use this power of movement independently, to enter into a player to effect tsukuri (*see* page 97). You can also use this power to move swiftly away from a player while holding him. This is essentially uki waza (*see* page 121).

ki hon no tsukuri develops independent power of movement, both from distance apart in atemi waza no uchikomi, and when holding a player's arm in kansetsu waza no hiji mochi no kuzushi (*see* page 160). Players can also develop i do ryoku through renzoku waza, or continuous application of technique. This means that when a player moves out of – or away from – a technique, you can follow it up with another one, which is logically determined by the stance he takes (shizentai no ri – aigamae/gyakugamae/jigotai, *see* page 41).

to itsu ryoku (Focusing Power in One Place)

to itsu ryoku is the ability to focus effort at a single anatomical point. From uke's point of view, this means allowing him to focus on a single anatomical point while you move around it. In this way, uke does not immediately register your evasive action. From tori's point of view, it means directing all your efforts towards a single weak point of uke's anatomy. This is a very important skill for aikidoka since aikido technique quintessentially exploits a single anatomical point. If you cannot focus your strength at one point, you may not be able to generate enough power to effect a technique.

Two exercises that develop to itsu ryoku in particular are sho tei awase and hi riki no yosei (*see* ki hon ko zo, pages 89–93). In these two exercises, you can see how to itsu ryoku can be used to move another player or to neutralize their power. In other words, it can be used in attack and defence.

datsu ryoku (Soft Arm Power)

datsu ryoku means 'to be drained of strength', and represents the power of softness. Perhaps one of the most important measures of the mastery of aikido technique, it involves the ability to take any stiffness out

of the body and to move with fluidity. Muscular strength is gauged by the amount of resistance against which the muscle can contract. If the resistance is taken away, the muscle relaxes. Therefore, an opponent's muscles will at best fixate to maintain a natural shape in the skeletal structure, which requires minimum effort. In other words, if you relax when you are grabbed, your attacker will not brace himself against an attack he does not perceive. It is then far easier to initiate tsukuri.

When using datsu ryoku in applying technique, the joints remain soft; it is often said that the elbow is absented from the arm, with the whole arm acting like a piece of rubber piping. Being struck by a piece of rubber piping is as effective as any punch! It also means that you can attach yourself via the arm to

Fig 329 Soft hand in grip.

Fig 330 Using soft arm for kuzushi.

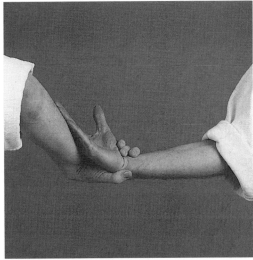

Fig 331 Soft hand.

your opponent's grip and move him by creating inertia.

Notice in Fig 331 that the hand sits flat inside uke's grip making a single arm.

to itsu ryoku can be used to neutralize power, datsu ryoku can be used to break balance and i do ryoku can be used to create tsukuri.

datsu ryoku can be used in applications of both atemi and kansetsu techniques. In this instance it is finished with oshi taoshi.

The most skilled randori players are those who can soften as well as harden their muscles at will. This is particularly important when applying kaeshi waza in randori. kaeshi waza is not applied using strength, but is applied at the moment toshu is at his weakest, which is at the moment he attempts to break balance. At this point, tanto must be soft in

Fig 332 to itsu ryoku.

Fig 333 datsu rokyo.

Fig 334 i do ryoku.

Fig 335 Resisting pull.

Fig 336 Resisting push.

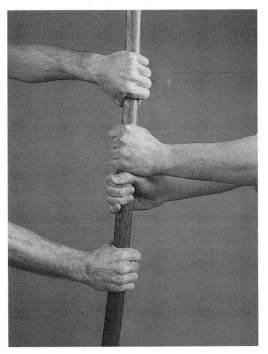

Fig 337 Holding stick.

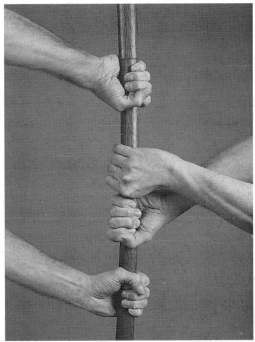

Fig 338 Rotating hands.

order to be receptive to the moment. The moment lasts just a split second, so players must train to 'see' it. This hardening and softening can be developed by resisting against a pull using floppiness and then switching quickly to a fixated shape to resist a push, and repeating the exercise.

If a player grabs your wrist with both hands, you can remain soft and manipulate his arms by turning them about the axis of the gripping hands. This principle can be seen clearly in Figs 337 and 338. Someone holds a stick with both hands; no matter how hard they grip the stick, if another person takes the stick at the top and bottom, they can easily turn it. The same principle can be applied when someone grabs your wrist or clothing.

This is a combination of to itsu ryoku and datsu ryoku which can also be combined

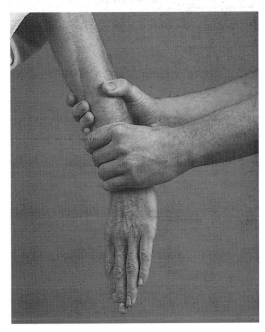

Fig 339 Holding wrist.

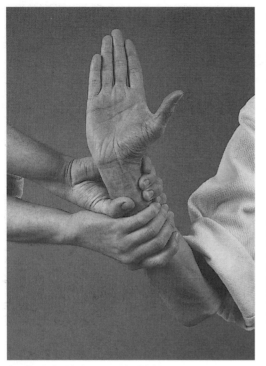

Fig 340 Rotating hands.

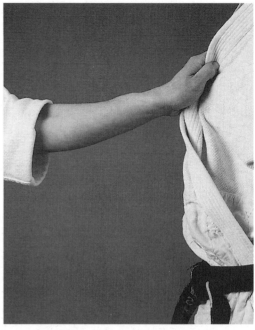

Fig 341 Holding gi.

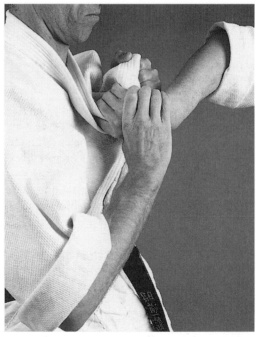

Fig 342 Rotating hands.

with i do ryoku to create very powerful balance breaks.

tegatana no kuzushi (Use of Handblade to Break Balance)

The tegatana can be used to break a player's balance. Generally, the use of tegatana to break balance is developed in the nana hon no kuzushi and hachi hon no kuzushi (*see* pages 93–6). There are also applications of these basic forms, some of which are demonstrated in the goshin ho 6th and 7th dan syllabuses.

For example, Fig 343 demonstrates a combination of both a tegatana chudan kuzushi and a tegatana gedan kuzushi, which, when accompanied with a kaiten turning i do ryoku, becomes a very powerful throw.

Fig 343 chudan/gedan kuzushi.

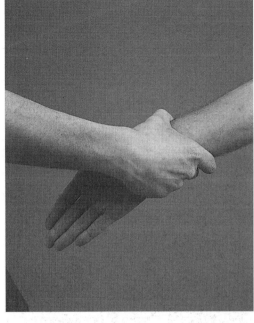

Fig 344 aigamae katate dori.

ri datsu ho
(Ability to Break Grip)

ri datsu is the ability to break out of grips. This ability can be utilized by a player when he is gripped by either the right or left hand. If you are gripped in aigamae (across grip), you can break grip easily by lifting your thumb as if hitching a lift. This action attacks the weakest part of the grip, which is where the thumb and index finger of the attacker's hand meet.

If you are gripped in gyakugamae (straight grip), you can break the grip easily by pushing your elbow towards that of the attacking arm.

Although these methods can be used to break grip, once we have broken the grip, the attacker may attack again. There are three

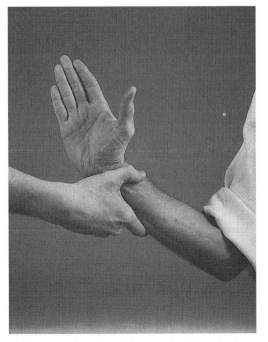

Fig 345 Breaking grip.

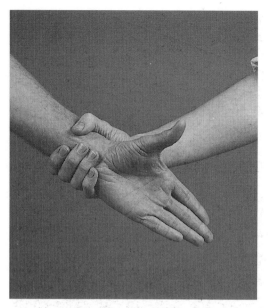

Fig 346 gyakugamae katate dori.

Fig 347 Breaking grip.

ways to control the gripping hand. The first is to use an atemi striking technique as soon as the grip has been broken. This is used, for example, in gyakugamae katate dori gedan ate.

In Fig 346, uke has grasped tori's hand with gyakugamae junte dori. tori has broken the grip and at the same time entered into uke and created a chance for gedan ate.

The second way to control the gripping hand is to take hold of it with the free hand as the grip is broken.

In Fig 349, uke has grabbed with aigamae katate dori. tori has taken hold of the gripping hand with the free hand, broken balance and broken grip. The forearm of the gripped hand is then pushed against the back of the hand as the gripped hand comes free, leading into kote gaeshi. This is the kote gaeshi technique for 8th kyu aigamae katate dori tekubi waza.

The third way to control the gripping hand while breaking the grip is nigiri kaeshi. Grip is broken and a grip is taken with the same hand. nigiri kaeshi can be applied from

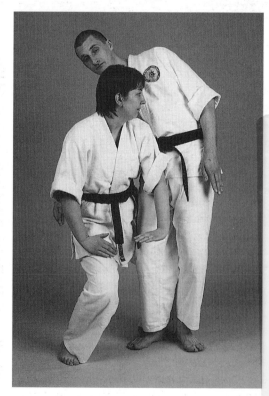

Fig 348 Into gedan ate.

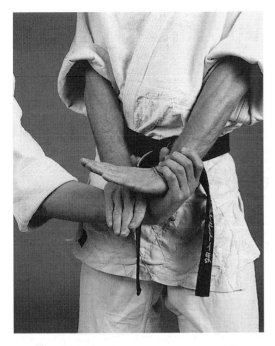

Fig 349 kuzushi.

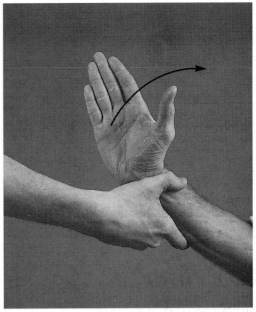

Fig 350 Breaking grip.

aigamae and gyakugamae junte dori using gyakute dori. The grip can be broken at jodan, or high level, and gedan, or low level. When the free hand is added to the grip to create circular grip, there are two opportunities to break balance at jodan, or high level, and two at gedan, or low level. These four possible gyakute dori grips are covered in the 3rd and 2nd kyu syllabuses when practising hontai no tsukuri nigiri kaeshi. The possible circular grips are practised in the 1st kyu hiji mochi no kuzushi requirement.

It takes many years of continuous practice to attain a combined understanding of to itsu ryoku, i do ryoku, datsu ryoku and ri datsu ho as they apply to aikido technique in both kata and randori, along with an understanding of the three principles of shizentai, ju and kuzushi, with all that is contained in them. This is the do of aikido.

Fig 351 Keeping contact on hand.

将来

8 The Future of Shodokan Aikido

Tomiki sensei was a great educator and he studied aikido from an educator's perspective. As a consequence, his is one of the most systemized forms of aikido. Tomiki wanted to leave nothing to chance or to suspended belief. Everything that he saw and experienced in aikido he sought to explain by contemporary philosophical, psychological and physiological theories. This was a deliberate attempt to place research of budo into a modern context. Much of his work was done at Waseda University in Tokyo; like Jigoro Kano before him, Tomiki saw the universities as a prime breeding ground for young fresh talent. For Tomiki, education and aikido were inseparable activities. In modern times, physical education is delivered primarily through sport, so Tomiki believed that the 'sportification' of aikido was necessary to ensure that its educational values were not lost.

In Japan, many students begin their practice of shodokan aikido at university and over a typical four-year degree course they may attain the level of 2nd dan. By this time they will already have significant competition experience. After graduation many join the labour market, and work obligations then greatly restrict their opportunities for aikido practice. A few will continue their practice and reach 3rd dan and an exceptional handful may be selected as uchi-deshi and continue through 4th and 5th dan. However, the vast majority leave college at 2nd dan, and subsequently find continuous aikido practice

difficult. Tomiki sensei was aware of this when he developed his system within the university scene, which is why there is a strong emphasis on the ki hon no kata, up to and including 3rd dan. Tomiki wanted students to leave university with a basic knowledge of aikido technique and a working understanding of timing and kuzushi.

In England, the university scene is largely untapped in respect of competitive aikido. The majority of adult participants are in employment, and have begun aikido practice later than the average Japanese. In England, there tends to be a period between the ages of 17 and 25 when many young people do not participate in sports. This is largely due to three factors: a sudden loss of the free facilities that school provides, social immaturity (it takes courage to walk into an established club as a total beginner at the age of 19), and a lack of financial independence. This trend is reflected in the average age of participants at competitions in the UK, in comparison with those in Japan. The world championships in Japan are dominated by some 300 Japanese students, with an average age of around 20. The average age of the British team will be closer to 30; 20-year-olds in the squad will have nowhere near the competitive experience of a Japanese student of the same age.

However, in England, because members tend to come to aikido practice once they are socially mature and financially independent, their practice remains on the whole unbroken, but less intense. The employed person's wants and needs in terms of the type of practice they are looking for often differ greatly from those of the full-time student. Both Kano and Tomiki recognized that young people hungered for competition and developed fighting systems, which would channel their youthful spirit and aggression. However, the student is not unduly concerned with loss of earnings should an injury occur during competition. It was on the 'battlefield' of fiercely fought campus competition that techniques that resulted in too many sprains or broken bones were revised, or removed. This made it the perfect environment for Tomiki to develop his system of competitive aikido.

The Japanese are not burdened with a perceived need for practical skills for self-defence. Japan is probably the safest advanced nation in the world. Consequently, for those Japanese who choose to practise the shinbudo of postwar Japan, the over-riding perception is one of participation in a sports or spiritual activity. In the UK, the opposite tends to be true and participants are often testing their aikido in respect of self-defence, since they constantly percieve the possibility of personal physical danger. However, aikido is not preoccupied with matters of self-defence. It is a study of timing, or kuzushi, and acquiesence on the psychological and physical plane, which may result in a partner, an opponent or an attacker being controlled or thrown. The end result may be of practical use in self-defence but the means is without predetermination or moral judgement – mu shin mu gamae.

Consequently, the Japanese student of competitive aikido tends to be more liberated in his practice, which makes learning a much easier and faster process.

randori and shiai are activities for young people. randori and shiai in competition are tools by which youngsters can learn many skills, both social and physical, which will enrich their lives in the long term. By the time these young people reach 3rd dan, many of these lessons and skills will be near completion, and may be carried on into a lifelong study of aikido. Tomiki himself maintained that competitive aikido was just one component of aikido. Over-emphasizing the competitive aspects of practice may indicate a lack of understanding of how the skills gained from such practice should be applied to further aikido study. Young people are keen to participate alongside their peers who share similar competitive experience, and competitive aikido is an exciting sport. This is why universities in the UK, where facilities are generally adequate and cheap, would be an excellent arena in which to develop competitive aikido. The best of the young players may become champions and instructors of the future.

At some point in the future, the Japan Aikido Association may attempt to put aikido forward as a possible Olympic demonstration sport. Tomiki sensei was highly influenced by Kano Jigoro, who was the first Asian to sit on the International Olympic Committee and it would be a wonderful achievement for all those dedicated to Tomiki to see the competitive element of his aikido accepted as an Olympic event alongside judo. Certainly, Tomiki agreed with Pierre de Coubertin's principle of combat among different nations in a sports arena, as a means of mutual understanding and in the interest of international harmony.

Bibliography

Alter, Michael J., *Science of Flexibility* (Human Kinetics Publishers Inc., 1996)

Coe, Sebastian, *More Than a Game* (BBC Books, 1992)

Friday, Karl F., *Legacies of the Sword* (University of Hawaii Press, 1997)

Kretchmar, R S., *From Test to Contest: philosophic inquiry in sport* (Human Kinetics Publishers Inc., 1988)

Lissner, H., *Biomechanics of Human Motion* (Saunders, 1962)

Nariyama, Tetsuro, *Shodokan Aikido Dojo 30th Anniversary* commemorative magazine (Ko Sei Press, 1997)

Pranin, Stanley A., 'Aikido Masters', *Aiki News* magazine, 1993

Pranin, Stanley A., 'Kano Jigoro', *Aiki News* magazine, 1990

Roberts, Tristan D.M., *Understanding Balance – the mechanics of posture and locomotion* (Chapman and Hall, 1995)

Shishida, Fumiaki, and Nariyama, Tetsuro, *Aikido kyoshitsu*, Sports V course (Dai Shu Kan Sho Ten, 1985)

Suzuki, Daisetsu T., *Sengai, the Zen Master* (Faber and Faber, London, 1971)

Tomiki, Kenji, *Aikido Nyumon* (Baseball magazine Co., first edition 1958)

Budo Ron (Dai Shu Kan Sho Ten, 1991)

Wildish, Paul, Various articles on Tomiki Kenji, *Aikido Review*, circa 1995

Useful Contacts

hombu dojo
Nariyama Shihan
1-28-9 Hannan cho
Abeno Ku
Osaka Shi 545
Japan

London shodokan
P. Newcombe 6th Dan
City University
Northampton Square
London EC2
UK
UK shodokan website:
www.gn.apc.org/shodokan/

Kyogikan
S. Allbright 4th Dan
Trafalgar Works
Trafalgar Street
Sheffield S1 1JD
UK
website: www.kyogikan.freeserve.co.uk
email: scott@kyogikan.freeserve.co.uk

British Aikido Association
www.aikido-baa.org.uk

USA Shodokan division
www.tomiki.org/main.html

Australian Shodokan division
www.staff.vu.edu.au/parla/tomiki.htm

www.aikiweb.com is a useful aikido directory that advertises books too.

Index